8/9/06
For Katherine, the best neighbor in the world! With gratitude and hugs,
Cathy

TALKING WITH GOD

Talking with God

Victor Books is an imprint of ChariotVictor Publishing
Cook Communications, Colorado Springs, CO 80918
Cook Communications, Paris, Ontario
Kingsway Communications, Eastbourne, England

Editor: Barbara Williams
Designer: Andrea Boven
Cover Photo: FPG, International; Laurance B. Aiuppe
Electronic Production: Elizabeth MacKinney

ISBN: 1-56476-608-X
Suggested Subject Heading: PRAYERS

Printed in the United States of America.

1 2 3 4 5 6 7 8 9 10 Printing/Year 01 00 99 98 97

INTRODUCTION

Since the first recorded communication of man to God, a sheepish "I heard You in the garden, and I was afraid because I was naked," we humans have used and abused this astonishing privilege. That God would create us with the capacity for fellowship with Him—even desire that fellowship—is a truth too wonderful to fully absorb.

But how do we communicate with God? Jesus Christ has already cracked the barriers between our myopic, one-dimensional, time-bound existence to the unimaginable realms of the Most High. But, what language do we use?

Whether it be the prayers of the great mystics who often communicated more in silent adoration than in words, or the simple "God bless Mommy and Daddy" of a child, God seems to be more concerned with our desire to communicate with Him than with the way we do it. Except for the prayer Jesus taught His disciples, Scripture mostly exhorts us to *pray.* Richard Foster says in *Prayer: Finding the Heart's True Home,* that the key to God's heart is prayer, and "the Father's heart is open wide you are welcome to come

in . . . overwhelming love invites a response. . . . With simplicity of heart we allow ourselves to be gathered up into the arms of the Father and let Him sing His love song over us."

This book is a collection of the prayers of the known and the unknown—the great and the small. It's a slice of the life of prayer of all kinds of people down through the ages. Perhaps you will see yourself in some of the prayers. Perhaps you will be freed up to be yourself in prayer as you've never been before—to trust that great Father love that opened the way for us to communicate directly with Him through the sacrifice of His Son, our Lord Jesus Christ.

For you did not receive a spirit that makes you a slave again to fear, but you received the Spirit of sonship. And by Him we cry, "Abba, Father."

Romans 8:15 (NIV)

"You have made us for Yourself, and our heart is restless until it rests in You." [1]

St. Augustine

Augustine grew up in a Christian home, but threw aside Christianity in his youth and sampled the pleasures of the wild side of Carthage where he was in school. Later, in Milan, he returned to Christianity under the influence of St. Ambrose, Bishop of Milan. He realized that his search for pleasure and meaning in life had finally found a resting place in Jesus Christ.

"O my God! in holy awe I bow before Thee, the Three in One. Again I have seen how the mystery of prayer is the mystery of the Holy Trinity. I adore the Father who ever hears, and the Son who ever lives to pray, and the Holy Spirit, proceeding from the Father and the Son, to lift us up into the fellowship of that ever-blessed, never-ceasing asking and receiving. I bow, my God, in adoring worship, before the infinite condescension that thus, through the Holy Spirit, takes us and our prayers into the Divine Life, and its fellowship of love." [2]

ANDREW MURRAY

Andrew Murray, the beloved South African turn-of-the-century preacher, wrote many books, but his most enduring is *With Christ in the School of Prayer*. In it he says, "Christ is our life. . . . It is when we believe this, and go and abide in Him for our prayer life too, that our fears of not being able to pray aright will vanish, and we shall joyfully and triumphantly trust our Lord to teach us to pray."

"I have nothing to do, now, but to please Thee.
And Thou art not hard to please,
O blessed Lover of us all." [3]

AMY CARMICHAEL

Irish missionary Amy Carmichael prayed this prayer when she found herself hopelessly bedridden after a fall at age sixty-four. By then Dohnavur Fellowship, her mission to temple children in India, was well established. Before her accident, on that same day, she had prayed, "Do with me as Thou wilt, do ANYTHING, Lord, that will fit me to serve Thee and help my beloveds." For the next twenty years until her death, Amy Carmichael was confined to bed, often in excruciating pain. But through her concentrated prayer, her letters, and the thirteen books she wrote, God used her in a far wider sense than she could ever have imagined.

"Thank You, Jesus . . . for laying me down and waking me up, and for the activities of my limbs. Lead and guide me through this day. Protect me from all harm and danger."

RUTH LOVE

At Progressive Peoples' Church in Chicago, Ruth Love is known as "Mother Love" and has often preached at the early morning service on Sundays. She is also known as the woman who organized a Bible study for children called "Operation Sunbeam" in the Robert Taylor Homes. This prayer is on her lips each morning when she wakes.

"Take me and use me, dear Father, without any of the old reservations." [4]

SAMUEL M. SHOEMAKER

Shoemaker prayed this prayer as a young man serving a short term assignment in the Far East. He'd spent much time wrestling with God about his future and whether he could leave it entirely in God's hands. Later, God greatly blessed his ministry in an Episcopal parish in New York City which put him in touch with the down-and-out as well as the well-to-do. In both stratas of society he saw the great need for healing from the disease of alcoholism, and helped found Alcoholics Anonymous. The first chapter of that organization met in a room in his church building.

"Dear Jesus, I don't know what I've gotten us into, but I really do pray for Ace. And I do pray right now that You'll show him—in some way he'll recognize—that You're listening to his prayer . . ."[5]

PAT BOONE

Ace, a pornographer with four failed marriages had just been told he needed a gallbladder operation. Scared, he asked Pat Boone to pray for him. Pat agreed, but encouraged Ace to pray himself. "Me? Pray? You gotta be kidding," Ace scoffed. God would never want to hear from him. Pat told Ace to talk to God like he was talking now—and ask for a sign that God heard him. Two days later, Ace called. "Lemme tell you what happened . . . the gallstones are gone!" The presurgery X rays showed no gallstones present. "But what do I do now?" Get a modern language Bible, Pat advised. "You know now that He's listening to you, don't you?" "Yeah. Yeah! I can dig it!" Ace hung up to go find a Bible.

"Lord, I can't think of anything else to say." [6]

EUGENIA PRICE

Early in her new life as a Christian, novelist, Eugenia Price, found herself on her knees every day, trying to "whip up" enough faith to pray effectively for her loved ones. Fervently, she pleaded with the Lord, outlining in detail how her prayers might be answered. No answers came. Then one day, exhausted, she admitted to God that she had given it all she had, and it wasn't enough. "Good," she sensed God saying. From that point, Eugenia's prayers changed from *her* work to *God's* work. "Suddenly I realized that He Himself is my faith too!" It was then that she began experiencing answered prayer.

"O Lord, Thou knowest how busy I must be this day. If I forget Thee, do not Thou forget me."

Lord Ashley

One of British General William Howe's men, Lord Ashley, is said to have prayed this prayer in 1777 before charging George Washington's troops in the battle of Edge Hill. The battle went to the British, but Howe later retreated when he realized Washington's troops could not be displaced.

"The Lord be blessed, the Lord be praised, who hath thus honored us, and strengthened us to suffer for His name's sake . . . Lord, lay not this sin to their charge." [7]

MARY FISHER

Mary Fisher had already spent sixteen months in prison for being so bold as to speak to her parish minister about her Quaker beliefs. In 1653, in the company of another Quaker woman, she began preaching to students at Sidney Sussex College in England. The town mayor acted quickly when he heard this. He had the women stripped to the waist and publicly whipped until their flesh was bleeding and torn. Instead of breaking under the torture, Mary invoked the Lord's blessing and even forgave the examiner since he was only doing what he was told to do.

"If, O Lord, You wish to me a fresh spectacle before men and angels, may Your holy will be done." [8]

Mme. Jeanne Guyon

She could have led a life of luxury and ease, but Mme. Guyon chose to live what she believed—that she was on earth to glorify God and to be wholly obedient to His will. She was acquainted with King Louis XIV and his wife. She associated with high churchmen. But after her husband died she felt called to travel throughout France, teaching people how to pray and telling them that true Christianity was a matter of the heart—an inner relationship with Christ. Her increasing popularity with the people lead jealous church leaders to accelerate a campaign against her which ended with her imprisonment in the Bastille.

"Lord, open the King of England's eyes." [9]

WILLIAM TYNDALE

As an English scholar, Tyndale provoked the wrath of bishops and royalty with his knowledge of Scripture. When he translated the Bible into English and published it for the masses, he marked himself for martyrdom. Tyndale was burned at the stake in 1536, calling out this prayer.

"O Lord, drench us with humility." [10]

OSWALD CHAMBERS

During weekly prayer meetings at Rye Chapel in London, fifteen-year-old Oswald Chambers found the courage to pray out loud. When he did, this prayer was one he frequently prayed. Oswald's reticence to pray in public did not come from lack of prayer experience. When he was only five, his family noticed how original his prayers were, and would sometimes listen outside his room at night as he knelt praying beside his bed. Chambers is best remembered for his classic devotional book, *My Utmost for His Highest*.

"Give me sunshine.
Give me Beauty.
Give me Pride. . .
Tell me that the beauty inside me
is what people see and love
instead of what they expect, project, and desire.
You are my Creator.
Help me find a way to love what You made." [11]

RACHEL DICKERSON

An ongoing battle with anorexia nervosa gave this young Washington, D.C. woman a new appreciation for herself as a unique creation of God.

"But oh God, tenderly, tenderly. Already, month by month and week by week You broke her body on the wheel whilst she still wore it. Is it not yet enough?" [12]

C.S. Lewis

C.S. Lewis was devastated by the loss of his wife, Joy Davidman, to cancer. As he worked through his grief, he found himself questioning the very foundations of his faith, contemplating what *really* was happening to his loved one on the other side. Was God still at it, tempering her soul, scouring the stains to perfection? If so, let it be with tenderness, he prayed.

"O Jesus, Master and Center and End of all, how long before that Glory is Thine which has so long waited Thee? Now there is no thought of Thee among men; then there shall be thought for nothing else. Now other men are praised; then none shall care for any other's merits. Hasten, hasten, Glory of Heaven, take Thy crown, subdue Thy kingdom, enthrall Thy creatures." [13]

JIM ELLIOT

This prayer was found in Jim Elliot's diary after he, with four other missionaries, was martyred in the Ecuador jungles in 1956.

"I make it my earnest prayer that God will keep you in His holy protection; that He would incline the hearts of the Citizens to cultivate a spirit of subordination and obedience to Government, and to entertain a brotherly affection and love for one another, for their fellow Citizens of the United States at large." [14]

President George Washington

At the Battle of Monongohela, the young recruit, George Washington, gained respect for his leadership when General Braddock was mortally wounded. Washington organized the rear guard and held back the French and Indians long enough for the wilting Federal troops to escape. The soldiers buried Braddock in a nearby forest. Since the chaplain was wounded too badly to officiate, Washington walked up to the grave, pulled a prayer book out of his coat, and read the appropriate Scripture and prayer. His prayer for the nation was equally appropriate, and came after he was elected President.

"I receive Thee, Price of my redemption . . . for love of whom I have studied and watched, toiled, preached, and taught. Never have I said anything against Thee; but if I have done so, it is through ignorance, and I do not persist in my opinions . . ."[15]

Thomas Aquinas

His stout figure and slow manner earned Thomas Aquinas the nickname, "Dumb Ox." But his quick mind earned him respect and position as a theologian and philosopher in the mid-1200s. Aquinas' writings reveal a man whose total being was in touch with God in a way few have experienced. At the end of his life, he asked to be served with the bread and wine of the Eucharist. When it arrived, he fell to the floor and prayed this prayer.

"Why, God? Why?"[16]

John Perkins

Dr. Robert Odenwald was one of the first white ministers in Mendenhall, Mississippi to show interest in John Perkin's Voice of Calvary ministry. A few months after their first meeting, Robert Odenwald committed suicide. The cost of preaching love and concern for black Americans to an all-white congregation was more than he could bear.

"Lord, I would like to put a fleece before You now. Here we are ready to do Your will if we can just find out what it is. Lord, if You want us to stay here in Philipsburg, we ask that You let us know by having the Committee vote for us unanimously. And let them decide of their own accord to fix up the parsonage with a decent refrigerator and stove. . . . And, Lord, let them volunteer to get rid of those cockroaches." [17]

Gwen and David Wilkerson

The congregation of the tiny Pennsylvania mountain church showed them the parsonage with its cockroaches and broken down refrigerator and stove . . . and young David Wilkerson and his wife, Gwen, prayed. Now, after their meeting, they approached the Wilkersons. "Reverend and Mrs. Wilkerson," began the chairman of the Committee, "we've taken a vote and everyone agrees that we want you to be our new pastor. Hundred percent. If you decide to come, we'll fix up the parsonage with a new stove and things, and Sister Williams says we'll have to fumigate the place."
"To get rid of those cockroaches," added Mrs. Williams.

"Precious Heavenly Father, I come to You with a grateful heart today because You have said that You are not willing that any should perish, but that all should come to repentance. So I boldly approach Your throne on behalf of my children and my sister. I ask that in Your mercy and Your grace that You continue to draw them to Yourself. May Your Holy Spirit speak to their hearts this day. May they be aware of Your presence and drawn by Your love. I thank You for Your faithfulness. I commit my loved ones to You in perfect confidence that Your will shall be done in their lives."

MABEL WILLIAMS

The "Grandma" of Arleta Richardson's *In Grandma's Attic* books prayed every day for the salvation of her children and her sister. Mabel never doubted that God would answer her prayer. Although she did not live to see this prayer answered, in time, each of them did commit their lives to Jesus Christ.

"Dear God, thank You for the good night's sleep—and for the terrific dream. I dreamed that we had a giant water slide in our backyard and a wave pool—a huge one just for me. It was just like the ocean. And I'm thankful we get to go to the zoo today. And please don't let me have to sit by a girl on the bus. And please help the mynah bird to talk to me." [18]

Kevin Kuzma, Age 9

For several years, Kevin's bedtime prayers had been a repeat of a few memorized words. His mother, Kay, tried to help him understand that God was his very best friend. "Don't you think He might like to hear something new something that's really important—like the things you tell your best friends?" she asked one night. Kay knew Kevin had gotten the message when he offered this table grace at breakfast the next morning.

"O Lord, may I be directed what to do and what to leave undone; and then may I humbly trust that a blessing will be with me in my various engagements. . . . Enable me, O Lord, to feel tenderly and charitably toward all my beloved fellow mortals . . ."[19]

ELIZABETH FRY

Elizabeth Fry was not prepared for the horrors of London's Newgate prison when she was granted permission to visit the women there in 1813. Three hundred women and their children with few clothes and no beds crowded four small rooms. This was the beginning of Elizabeth Fry's prison ministry and advocacy for prison reform. The Lord answered this, her constant prayer, by giving her influence throughout the British Isles and Europe.

"Lord, take him to Scarborough and Ireland, and Scotland, and bring him back to us laden with souls." [20]

Reader Harris

Shortly after becoming engaged to Miss Biddy Hobbs in the fall of 1908, Oswald Chambers left for three months of speaking engagements sponsored by the League of Prayer. His respected mentor and founder of the League, Reader Harris, sent him on his way with this prayer. It was the last time Oswald saw Reader Harris alive.

"Lord, I'm ready. I don't know where this is going to take me, but I'm ready. We can go back to the beginning now." [21]

CAROLYN KOONS

For years Carolyn Koons had lived with the sometimes buried memories of unbelievable childhood abuse from both father and mother. She knew she needed healing of her inner pain. God was simply waiting until she was willing to face the painful memories—from the beginning. At this point, the healing began.

"O God, You know how those Aucas killed our beloved Senor Eduardo, Senor Jaime, and Senor Pedro. O God, You know that it was only because they didn't know You. They didn't know what a great sin it was. They didn't understand why the white men had come. Send some more messengers, and give the Aucas, instead of fierce hearts, soft hearts. Stick their hearts, Lord, as with a lance. They stuck our friends, but You can stick them with Your Word, so that they will listen, and believe." [22]

QUICHUA INDIAN CHRISTIANS

In January of 1956, Christians everywhere were stunned with the news of the slaying of five American missionaries by Auca Indians they were attempting to reach in the jungles of Ecuador. Three of the men, Ed McCully, Jim Elliot, and Pete Fleming, worked with Quichua Indians who came to know God through their ministry.

"Here in the presence of Almighty God, we kneel in silence, and with penitent and obedient hearts confess our sins, so that we may obtain forgiveness by your infinite goodness and mercy. Amen." [23]

THE BOOK OF COMMON PRAYER

Since its publication in 1789, *The Book of Common Prayer* has helped countless people around the world to communicate their thoughts and feelings to God.

"We do this work as Your servants and in Your service. If we can't do it for lack of money, it is Your cause which suffers. What profit is there in my death . . . will the dust praise Thee? There will be one soul less in this world to serve and praise You and, by the way, there aren't too many of us left."[24]

CORRIE TEN BOOM

In the middle of a meeting of Dutch resistance workers in the ten Boom home during World War II, Corrie ten Boom interrupted the discussion. "Listen, we've run out of money," she said. "There are some people here who need it desperately. Will you join me in praying. . . ?" The startled group obediently folded their hands and closed their eyes as Corrie prayed. Before she finished, the doorbell rang. It was a messenger delivering an envelope containing 500 guilders!

"Refresh me, Lord. Refresh me." [25]

RICHARD J. FOSTER

In his book, *Prayer, Finding the Heart's True Home,* Richard Foster tells about paddling over to a small island to find solitude during a conference in Canada. After praying for the refreshment of spirit he needed, Foster sensed that God's words to him for the day were, "Be still . . . Rest . . . Shalom"—simple, profound, refreshing, from the gentle and caring heart of his Heavenly Father.

"Over three hundred and thirty millions who cannot read are calling for help. Need is Your language, is a word from You. How to approach this problem is baffling. Unsolved problems are Your language, for in them You are our schoolmaster training us."[26]

FRANK LAUBACH

Laubach wrote this prayer as he observed the crowded Baroda Bazaar in India. His passion for gifting people with the ability to read in their own language sent him all over the world, teaching his methods. It was on the Philippine island of Mindanao that Laubach realized the power of this gift. As a Presbyterian missionary, he had come to the island to reach the primitive Moro tribe who seemed to resist any attempts to get to know them. His ministry took on exciting dimensions when he learned their language, and began teaching them to read and write.

"Lord, I know the power You have to solve problems, to heal and to give peace. I have turned this situation over to You, and I trust Your promises. The whole matter could be cleared up in less time than it takes to pray about it. I don't understand why it hasn't been."

ARLETA RICHARDSON

After moving her sister from one nursing care center to another, four times in five years, Arleta Richardson was forced to move her again. She decided it was time to have a serious talk with God. God's answer came quickly, "Will you trust Me, anyway?" The joy and peace Arleta had experienced from years of trust in her Heavenly Father made only one answer possible: "Yes!"

"O God, Thou puttest into my heart this great desire to devote myself to the sick and sorrowful. I offer it to Thee." [27]

FLORENCE NIGHTINGALE

The wealthy Nightingale family protested her plan to become a nurse and give her service to the needy. Nothing, not even several proposals of marriage, could dissuade Florence Nightingale from the path she was sure God had laid before her. In the mid-1800s, during the Crimean War, Florence Nightingale became the ministering angel who not only continued to check on wounded soldiers far into the night, but who understood organization and efficiency so well that she was made supervisor of all the hospitals in her area.

"Lord, forgive me, for Jesus' sake, and give me another chance, and I will go to England."[28]

AMANDA SMITH

The daughter of a slave, Amanda Smith learned early in life the riches of being God's child. Her desire was to evangelize, and she began traveling the country by rail, trusting God for safety, courage, and finances. Her ministry was so successful that she was given the opportunity to go to England with her message. To see herself mingling with people of means on a fine ocean steamer, and then with the British, took greater faith than trusting God for a new pair of shoes when all she had was a dime. She wasn't ready for such a trip. Then Amanda confessed her lack of trust, and agreed to go. The Lord blessed her ministry to England, using it as a stepping-stone to a new work in Africa.

"Another lump . . . O Father, not again . . . You know how frightening this is for me . . . this flood of fear . . . remember the last time we went through this, how scared I became? But You were there I'm trying to remember that . . . I must call the doctor right away." [29]

SUE MONK KIDD

Sue Monk Kidd's journey to discover God's love for her began with searing chest pains—an undeniable message to slow down—and the realization that for all her devoted work for God, she really didn't know Him. Her soul had never been quiet enough to hear Him. Slowly God's love began to be reality and she also discovered a new way of praying—keeping a running conversation with God. When she found a lump in her breast she says, "The conversation that ran on during the next few days brought me enormous peace, turning what might have been dark thoughts into an honest dialogue with God instead of a lonely monologue with myself."

"Dear Lord, I thank You that I have lost nothing this year. You have given me my seed back. Thank You!" [30]

Robert Schuller's Father

Only one field of corn had survived the devastating Midwest drought. An underground water source beneath the plot kept the corn growing and yielded a half a wagon of corn. Robert Schuller's father saw it as a gift from the Lord, for it would give them enough seed for their whole next year's planting. When the family gathered for dinner after the harvest, his father offered this prayer.

PETER MARSHALL

As they drove from Decatur to Atlanta after Catherine's last college exam, Peter Marshall's gratitude exploded. Catherine Wood had just accepted his marriage proposal. Peter had proposed earlier, but Catherine suggested that they pray about it for several days. She was now sure that God was in agreement with their desire to marry. After a long pause following his outburst, Peter stopped the car beside the road and prayed "an achingly beautiful prayer," as Catherine reported. "Only then did he take me into his arms."

"Grant, O merciful God, that with malice towards none, with charity for all, with firmness in the right as you give us to see the right, we may strive to finish the work we are in; to bind up the nation's wounds . . . to do all which may achieve and cherish a just and lasting peace among ourselves and with all nations; through Jesus Christ our Lord." [32]

President Abraham Lincoln

Abraham Lincoln never formally joined a church. He attended the church his wife belonged to and brought up his children in that denomination. But he was a student of the Bible and believed that he would never succeed as President without God's help and direction. Once he said, "When any church will inscribe over its altars its sole qualification for membership the Saviour's condensed statement of both Law and Gospel, *Thou shall love the Lord thy God with all thy soul, and with all thy mind: and thy neighbor as thyself,* that church will I join with all my heart and all my soul.

"God, I don't have any friends. I don't have anyone else to turn to. God, You're going to have to be my friend, my best friend. And You're going to have to tell me how to do things and give me wisdom, because I don't know what to do." [33]

SONJA CARSON

Faced with raising two boys on her own, poor reading skills, and never having worked for a salary, Sonja Carson sought help from the only one she knew could help her. God honored her determination to work as hard as she could and leave the rest up to Him. She taught her grade-school-age boys to take responsibility, worked two and three jobs at a time, and saved every penny she could, refusing to accept welfare. Today one of Sonja's sons is a successful engineer and the other is a pediatric neurosurgeon.

"Jesus Savior, Gentle Shepherd
Bless Thy little lamb tonight.
In the darkness be Thou near me
Keep me safe 'till morning light.

"All this day Thy hand has led me
And I thank Thee for Thy care.
Thou hast warmed me, clothed me, fed me.
Listen to my evening prayer."

DON MOELLER (SOURCE UNKNOWN)

Now in his seventies, Don Moeller has prayed this prayer every night since he was a child. The prayer is characteristic of Don's life of total trust in God. This trust held up during a physical testing when, after he retired as a Navy officer, a stubborn infection in his nasal passages almost took his life. It did take the sight in one eye. That has not stopped Moeller from studying the Bible with a group of fellow church members at Beautiful Savior Lutheran Church in Spokane, Washington for the past eighteen years!

"Jesus loves me—this our toast." [34]

ZAC HANSEL, AGE 2 1/2

After being taught the song, "Jesus Loves Me, This I Know," Zac folded his hands, bowed his head, and offered this prayer at the breakfast table.

"All right, Lord, You must have something else in mind. Could it possibly be something here in the United States? Perhaps something in the inner city?"[35]

Colleen and Louis Evans

There was no doubt in either of their minds that God had called them as missionaries to Africa. So when the mission board told Colleen and Louis Evans that they could only send medical people that year, they were bewildered. What did the Lord have in mind? Again, they were convinced it must be inner city work. Then it became clear that God wanted them in affluent Bel Air, California, ministering to the opposite end of the economic scale. The mansions and manicured lawns of Bel Air proved to be more of a mission field than they could have dreamed.

"Now, Lord, what shall I do? . . . Yes, Lord . . .
I will give You my all, all I know,
and all I don't know." [36]

E. Stanley Jones

A year after he had become a Christian, E. Stanley Jones faced a crisis in his relationship with Jesus Christ. God used a book, *The Christian's Secret of a Happy Life* by Hannah Whithall Smith, to bring him to a place where he could pray a prayer of relinquishment. From then on, he felt empowered by the Holy Spirit to be the person God wanted him to be. Jones became a missionary, a spiritual leader to generals and presidents, and an author whose books have inspired millions.

"Dear Lord, this Bible is my strength.
I can't wait to tell the truth!" [37]

JOHN GREENE

Attacked and beaten by two drunken white men, John Greene now had his chance to see justice done. At the trial, with his hand on the Bible, he was ready to testify against his assailants. But John Greene's commitment to living Jesus' way was stronger than his need for revenge. When the two men pleaded guilty, he asked the judge, "Is it possible for you to sentence the men to community service instead of jail?" The surprised judge agreed. After the sentencing, one of the men shook John's hand and said, "I'm sorry . . . I'll never forget what you've done for me."

"God, I don't know how to find You, but I'm going to try! I'm not much the way I am now, but somehow I want to give myself to You. Take me . . ." [38]

Charles Colson

Few would have expected Nixon's "hatchet man" to seek a born-again experience with Jesus Christ. But that's what Charles Colson did in 1973 on a hot and humid New England evening. The Christian witness and compassion of his host and friend, Tom Phillips, shook him to his core. Tom gave him a copy of *Mere Christianity* by C.S. Lewis and urged him to also read the Book of John. As Charles Colson drove away from Phillips' home that night, tears of relief forced him off the road. Sobbing, he prayed his first real prayer.

"Defend, O Lord, this Thy child with Thy heavenly grace, that she may continue Thine forever." [39]

Confirmation prayer for Frances Ridley Havergal

The author of the hymn, "I Gave Myself for Thee," and many others, was influenced by her minister father who composed music for the cathedrals of England. On her confirmation day Frances Ridley Havergal felt the bishop's hands on her head and heard the words, "Thine forever." Her whole being responded to these words and set the tone for her future ministry in song.

"Lord, Thou art enough for me, just Thyself, without any of Thy gifts or Thy blessings. I have Thee and I am content. I will be content. I choose to be content. I am content." [40]

Hannah Whitall Smith

Just before she died in 1911, Hannah Whitall Smith penned this prayer, a testimony to her intimate relationship with God. Hannah is best known for *The Christian's Secret of a Happy Life,* a book still found in the homes of many believers today. She was born into a Quaker family, but her spirit was set on fire after she and her husband encountered a revival early in their marriage. Both of them occasionally preached at gatherings in America and in England.

"Lord, help me. I don't know how to die. I'm afraid. Give me the strength to die. Show me how." [41]

CAROL LOVELL

Alone in the restaurant where she worked, Carol Lovell was accosted by a man who shot her twice in the head. First she prayed that God would help her die. Instead, God infused her with the will to live, and Carol was able to stagger to a phone and call for help. Throughout her six months of recuperation, Carol knew the power of God's strength giving her hope and confidence for recovery.

"Thank You Lord. Thank You for sharing this beautiful life You've given me. Love," [42]

TEDDY BEAR

In the early 1980 s Edwina Gateley founded Genesis House, a ministry to prostitutes in Chicago. This is the prayer of one of the women whose life was touched by this ministry.

"Do You, my God, stand by me, against all the world's wisdom and reason. . . . I would prefer to have peaceful days and to be out of this turmoil. But Yours, O Lord, is this cause. . . . Stand by me, O God, in the name of Your dear Son, Jesus Christ, who shall be my Defense and Shelter, yes, my Mighty Fortress, through the might and strength of Your Holy Spirit. Amen." [43]

MARTIN LUTHER

Luther, who went from practicing law to the priesthood, continued to feel anxiety over the state of his soul. In 1513, while studying the New Testament in preparation for lectures at Wittenberg where he was a professor, Luther found his answer in the letters of Paul. "For by grace you have been saved, through faith . . ." His discovery of a loving God who promised salvation through faith in Jesus Christ, not because of works, revolutionized Luther's life. The nailing of his ninety-five controversial theses on the door of the palace church in 1517 revolutionized the church, and marked the first break in its unity.

"O Lord, I yield me to Thy grace,
Grant me mercy for my trespass;
Let never the fiend my soul chase.
Lord, I will bow and Thou shalt beat;
Let never my soul come in hell heat.
Into Thy hands I commend my spirit; Thou hast redeemed me, O Lord of truth." [44]

JOHN BROWNE

During the reign of King Henry VIII in England, John Browne was one of those burned at the stake for daring to question some of the practices and teachings of the church. Clamped in the stocks the night before he died, Browne told his wife, who was allowed to sit beside him, that two church officials had burned his feet to the bone on hot coals. "They did this," he told her, "to make me deny my Lord, which I will never do. . . I pray thee therefore, good Elizabeth, continue as thou hast begun, and bring up thy children virtuously and in the fear of God." The next day he yielded his soul to God at the burning stake.

"Lord, we know that You'll be coming through this line today, so help us to treat You well."

MARY GLOVER

Early Friday mornings, the Sojourners Neighborhood Center in Washington, D.C. prepares the morning food line. Before the doors open to the three hundred-some families the center feeds, volunteers, many of them the poor and needy themselves, join hands in prayer. Usually Mary Glover, an African American woman in her seventies, is the one who prays. Mary is familiar with Jesus' words in Matthew, "Whatever You did for one of the least of these brothers of Mine, you did for Me."

"Let us sing unto the Lord, for He hath been glorified exceedingly: the horse and the rider hath He thrown into the sea. He is become my helper and my shield unto salvation. Who is like unto Thee, O Lord, among the gods? Who is like Thee, glorious in holiness, marvelous in praises, doing wonders?"[45]

EMPEROR CONSTANTINE

Constantine the Great, ruler of the Roman empire in the 4th century A.D., became a Christian in his youth. At his decree as emperor, Christianity became the official religion of the empire. Constantine surrounded himself with priests of the church, convinced that peace and prosperity for the empire was dependent on God's power. After a battle outside Rome when his opponent's army was swept into the river and drowned like the Egyptians pursuing the Israelites, Constantine sang these ancient praises to God for victory, and marched triumphantly into the city.

"Thank You, God, for this wonderful creation of Yours. What could I give You back for it?" [46]

MARIA VON TRAPP

On a hiking trip in the high Alps, Maria felt her soul lift in gratitude while the sunset turned the sky from pink to red. Then, as she spread her arms wide and shouted this prayer, it occurred to her that what she could give back to God was what meant the most to her—climbing mountains and enjoying the wonders of nature. She would cloister herself in a convent. But God had other plans, and eventually led her out of the convent to a family of seven children who needed a mother and a song.

"Hold her gently in Thy hands
With love and warmth and tender care;
Hold her closely in Thy arms,
That she may find quiet comfort there." [47]

Dianne Ward

Dianne, twenty-one and just married, wrote this prayer for her mother who had just experienced one of the final crises in her long battle with cancer. Her mother, Alice Armstrong Ward, knew the power of prayer. For years she had been active in a prayer and healing ministry, and responsible for the forming of numerous prayer groups. God called her home at the age of fifty-five.

"Oh, God, give me strength for Jennifer and the baby . . ."

"Thank You, God! Daddy made it! Daddy made it!" [48]

JAMES STOLPA
JENNIFER STOLPA

En route from San Francisco to Idaho, Jennifer and James Stolpa and their infant son were lost in a blinding snowstorm. For three days they waited in their truck for help to arrive, then set out walking. After two days, Jennifer could go no further. She and the baby huddled in a cave in a sleeping bag while James set off again for help, desperately praying for strength. Three days later, after a truck driver picked up James, Jennifer joyfully welcomed a rescue party. Miraculously, though his parents suffered severe frostbite, the baby's only complaint was diaper rash.

"Whatever You desire, I desire. Whatever You will, I will as long as I live . . . I only ask that I love You with all my heart, all the days of my life. . . . You will give me the grace to carry on with joy and peace of heart, and someday You will carry me to the home I have longed for and dreamed about."

JOSIFINA GUERRERO

In the Philippines, during World War II, Josifina Guerrero disguised herself as an old woman and smuggled strategic plans directly through Japanese lines to the Americans. She received an award for her bravery from the President of the United States. Josifina suffered from leprosy, and was well acquainted with the One who gives courage and comfort to the weak.

"Lord, Make me a kite flying high
and free in a heavenly blue sky.
Teach me I cannot fly without wind.
As the pressure of a forceful wind
drives a delicate kite upward,
Let the pressures of my life push me
closer towards You.
Help me remember
when the stress of living blows in,
I can soar in growth.
I can float on faith.
And I will!"

PAT VERBAL

Between preparing budgets and keeping up with all the other duties of an associate pastor of a growing church, Pat Verbal juggled her role as a wife and mother of two active teenage boys. She felt the pressures mounting. During spring break, Pat hosted a "Kite Sunday" at church, presenting each child with a "Jesus Loves Me" kite. Later, during a rare hour of calm during lunch alone in a park, Pat reflected on this event, what it meant for children, and realized the Lord had a message in it for her. The prayer she wrote that day has given her focus and hope on many impossible days.

"You know, Lord, how well You know, the years when I didn't pray (or didn't think I prayed). How could I pray to Someone whose very existence I doubted. . . . Yet all the while I was hungering for You, groping to find Your hand as I stumbled in the darkness of my needs . . ."[49]

MARJORIE HOLMES

Marjorie Holmes struggled for years before she found God personal and real. One day a friend asked her, "Do you find God or does God find you?" "I don't care," Marjorie answered. "I just want us to find each other!" "Then, open the door," the friend said. "God wants you even more than you want Him . . . talk to Him. Use prayer." With that, Marjorie Holmes began talking to God as an ever-present friend. Since then, her books have encouraged people all over the world in their communication with God through Christ.

"I thank Thee, O God, for the relief and satisfaction of mind that come with the firm assurance that Thou dost govern the world; for the patience and resignation to Thy providence that are afforded as I reflect that even the tumultuous and irregular actions of sinful men are, nevertheless, under Thy direction, who art wise, good, and omnipotent, and hast promised to make all things work together for good to them that love Thee." [50]

SUSANNA WESLEY

Were it not for Susanna Wesley, there would have been no Charles or John. Susanna bore nineteen children. Ten died before they became adults, and of these, two claimed a firm place in religious history. John's fervor for piety, discipline, and evangelism led him to found the Methodist movement. Charles' hymns became the sound of early Methodism and are still sung in churches around the world. No doubt the one evening a week Susanna committed to each of her children for conversation and study impacted the rest of their lives.

"Use me, my Savior, for whatever purpose and in whatever way You may require. Here is my poor heart, an empty vessel: fill it with Your grace. Here is my sinful and troubled soul: quicken it and refresh it with Your love. Take my heart for Your abode; my mouth to spread abroad the glory of Your name; my love and all my powers for the advancement of Your believing people; and never allow the steadfastness and confidence of my faith to abate."[51]

DWIGHT L. MOODY

In the mid-1800s the tents and shanties of Chicago's neighborhoods sprawled in disarray beside cold Lake Michigan. Dwight L. Moody's concern for the disadvantaged of these neighborhoods, especially the children, moved this successful Chicago businessman to become a full-time urban missionary. Moody founded a Bible Institute for Home and Foreign Mission, confident that many of the young people who attended would volunteer for full-time Christian service. Today the school is known as The Moody Bible Institute.

"Well, here we are, Lord,
and we just haven't done the job. . . .
We meant to do better, but we've been so distracted.
I mean—there have been telephone calls
and the door bell, and the television . . .
and in the process, O Lord,
We haven't told the world about You.
Forgive us. We repent . . .
We are going to go out of here
and a revival will break out
and the fire will spread . . .
So Lord, we feel the power coming on."

DR. ROBERT SCHULLER

Robert Schuller offered this prayer on the second day of the Lausanne II International Congress on World Evangelization in 1989. The conference, held in Manila just six weeks after the shocking massacre in Beijing's Tiananmen Square, brought together 3,000 Christian leaders from 170 countries of the world. It followed by fifteen years the first Lausanne congress and evaluated and confirmed what participants agreed was the calling of the church—"to take the Gospel to the whole world."

"Oh Father . . . You desire mercy rather than judgment. Now be merciful to me, a sinner. And bless You for not judging me according to these awful thoughts. Stupid, silly thoughts that distract me from worshiping You. Be merciful and help me win this battle—for Your honor and for the benefit of this man, whoever he is . . ." [52]

Joni Eareckson Tada

During a Sunday morning service, Joni's attention was diverted from the sermon by the sight of a dark head of thick black hair on a man a few pews ahead. Joni reminded herself that she was in a wheelchair, a paraplegic, and resigned to being a thirty-something single. Then she refocused her thoughts on the Lord. Two years later the black-haired man, Ken Tada, and Joni Eareckson, were married.

"In Thee, O Lord, do I put my trust: let me never be put to confusion. Deliver me in Thy righteousness, and cause me to escape: incline Thine ear unto me, and save me. Be Thou my strong habitation, whereunto I may continually resort: Thou hast given commandment to save me; for Thou art my rock and my fortress." [53]

ETHEL WATERS (PSALM 71:1-3)

At one of the lowest points in her life, Ethel Waters prayed these words from the Psalms and gained the courage to go on. After great success as an actress and singer, Ethel found herself between jobs with her money dwindling. Alone in her starkly appointed hotel room, she looked to God and His Word—the Source that had already seen her through a life familiar with trouble and disappointment, as well as joy.

"God, there are other people that have more education than I have . . . Lord, I can't leave my family. I just can't do it. I just can't do it. I just can't accept the responsibility. I'm just not capable. I wasn't born to do that." [54]

Rev. Howard Southards

For three and a half years, Howard Southards tried to convince God that he was not preacher material. But God kept burdening him with the sense that his mission was to preach. Finally, when his wife joined the Lord in urging him to listen to his calling, he relented, praying, "Lord, I know I can't do much and I know there's others that could do a better job, but if You want me to go, here I am. I'm willing to do the best I can." Rev. Southards became a well-regarded Independent Baptist minister in Appalachia.

"God, You know how hard this is for me. My heart is breaking. Juliann is not going to make it. As her mother, I do not have the courage and strength to give her back to You right now. Please give me Your courage and strength. Hold me, Father, I come as a little child wanting to crawl up onto Your lap and just be held. I cannot walk this road alone. Lord, I want Your will for her life, whatever that may be."

SHERI BIGNELL

As Sheri prayed, kneeling beside the back seat of her van in the hospital parking lot, God's peace began to settle over her. Yesterday, her five-year-old daughter Juliann, was rushed to the hospital when she choked on her seizure medication. Now Juliann fought for her life in intensive care, hooked up to life support systems. In the days that followed, it was God's inexplicable peace that made it possible for Sheri to slowly relinquish her daughter and let her slip home to her Heavenly Father. Since their daughter's homegoing, Sheri and her husband have adopted a two-year-old girl who was abandoned by her mother.

"Lord, You always give Robert Schuller these great ideas. Could You give me just one?"[55]

BECKY TIRABASSI

Hungry for a new touch of God in her life, Becky Tirabassi decided to commit herself to one hour of prayer a day. She began by writing out her prayers and the Lord's response to them. Before long, she felt a growing need for a plan. She prayed for a way to be more accountable. Then the idea came to develop a notebook called "My Partner" for journaling prayer, praise, confession, and requests. The idea was also an answer to the continuing prayer of this young housewife to be used in the lives of others for God's glory. Thousands have purchased "My Partner" notebooks which Becky now prepares for others.

"O Lord, the Governor of all things, set bounds to our passions by reason, to our errors by truth, to our discontents by good laws justly executed, and to our divisions by charity. . . . Grant this, O God, in Your good time and for ever. . . . O Lord, make Your way plain before me. Let Your glory be my end, Your Word my rule; and then Your will be done." [56]

Charles I, King of England, Scotland, and Ireland

In spite of his request for God's guidance, Charles I's reign was a rocky one. He insulted the Protestants by marrying a Catholic princess. He angered the people with his choice of foreign minister and unfair taxes. He enraged the Scots by trying to force on them a new state church structure. Finally, during civil war with the Scots, Charles was captured and beheaded in 1649.

"Lord, my Savior, Thou standest at the door and wouldst enter in. O come, Thou beloved guest, for I desire to depart and be with Thee. Let my children be committed to Thy mercy. Lord, look down in mercy upon Thy church. May the pure doctrine which God has sent through my husband be handed down unadulterated to posterity." [57]

Katherine von Bora Luther

Six years after her husband, Martin, died, Katherine Luther talked with her Savior as she lay dying. After Martin's death, Katherine and her children lived through the war of Charles V against the Protestants, as well as the bubonic plague. Katherine's buoyant faith remained strong to the end. She had been Luther's support and unfailing cheerleader during their marriage. Luther never intended to marry, but when Katherine and eight other fugitive nuns descended on Wittenberg looking for refuge, she changed his mind. Luther sometimes referred to her as, "Kate, my rib."

"I'll do my best for You . . .
Please, God let me be Your servant."[58]

MARK, AGE 12

When child psychiatrist Dr. Robert Coles interviewed children around the world about their spiritual lives, he met a boy named Mark in Tennessee. Mark's athletic ability gave him a considerable edge in track competition. But what impressed Dr. Coles was Mark's attitude toward his success and God's part in it. "You can't say God wants you to win," Mark said. "He wants our faith in Him, and then we try our best." Before a race Mark didn't pray to win. He prayed to be God's servant.

"Lord, remember not only the men and women of good will, but also those of ill will. But do not remember all the suffering they have inflicted on us. Remember the fruits we have, thanks to these sufferings—the greatness of heart that has grown out of all of this—and when they come to judgment, let all the fruits we have borne be their forgiveness."[59]

RAVENSBRUCK PRISONER

This prayer—a superb model of forgiveness from the Holocaust—was found near the body of a dead child in Ravensbruck concentration camp.

"O God, show me the way through,
for I have no way to turn."[60]

HAZEL LEE

Life seemed to be closing in on her that year in India. Hazel Lee and her husband, Earl, had followed her grandparents' steps back to India as missionaries. Now Hazel was exhausted and both she and their baby son were ill. She tried to pray, but felt cut off from God. One day she handed Earl the baby and went into the bedroom to pray, desperate for help. On her knees, Hazel heard an inner voice directing her to a book on the bedside table with the single word title, *Rejoice.* The message she found there was life changing: delight in God for Himself alone, and He will come to your rescue.

"Kyrie eleison. Christe eleison. Lord have mercy. Christ have mercy. Lord have mercy."

The Kyrie

In Greek, *Kyrie* means "Lord," and *eleison* is the word for "have mercy." Some churches with a formal liturgy still include this ancient prayer which was used in the church during the first centuries. (Pronounced Ke'rea ala'eson, and kre'sta ala'eson.)

"Oh God, help me to decide what I should do now. I feel so very much alone to make this decision. Guide me and, if I should agree to go, give me the strength to do what they want me to do."

Master Sergeant Eleanor Bilby

In 1942, in the London headquarters of the United States Army, Eleanor Bilby was given a half hour to decide whether to pose as a member of the French underground. Though she spoke French fluently, she hadn't anticipated anything like this when she volunteered for the Women's Army Corps. Fortified with the commitment and courage of her faith, Eleanor agreed to go. Weeks later, she was hired as a secretary in the Gestapo headquarters office in Paris where she had access to information vital to the underground movement. Today Eleanor tutors children in the inner city.

"Dear Father in heaven,
We lift our first lady to You today. . . .
May she cultivate a forgiving heart, Lord, toward
all the hard things a first lady must endure . . .
May she become better and not bitter in adversity. . . .
May she and her family grow closer every day. . . .
And finally, dear Lord, when her job is done,
may she have that true peace and contentment of
knowing that she has been a good and
faithful steward in Your service.
Amen."

SUSAN BAKER

At the Presidential Prayer Day Luncheon in 1994, Susan Baker, wife of former Secretary of State Jim Baker, offered this prayer for Hillary Rodham Clinton.

"O Lord, I do not pray for tasks equal to my strength: I ask for strength equal to my tasks." [61]

PHILLIPS BROOKS

The six-foot-six-inch Philadelphia pastor loved children and kept his study full of toys and dolls. His other great interest, music, lead him to write hymns and store at least 200 in his memory. When he visited the Holy Land in 1865 he sent back letters to his young friends, describing what he saw. Brooks' well-known carol, "O Little Town of Bethlehem," was written after that trip.

"Lord God Almighty, I pray You for Your great mercy and by the token of the Holy Cross, Guide me to Your will, to my soul's need, better than I can myself; And shield me against my foes, seen and unseen; And teach me to do Your will that I may inwardly love You before all things with a clear mind and body. For You are my Maker and my Redeemer, my help, my comfort, my trust, and my hope. Praise and glory be to You, now, ever and ever, world without end." [62]

Alfred the Great, King of England

Both ill health and the Danes made most of King Alfred's life miserable. But his deep faith in God sustained him through battle after battle with the warring Danes. Because of King Alfred's penchant for learning, he revived interest in education. The scholars he gathered around him influenced the church, as regard for learning among the clergy increased. Ten years before his death in 899, King Alfred learned Latin and began to translate some of the classics.

"Our Heavenly Father, Thou who art the God of the macrocosm and the microcosm, of the infinite and the infinitesimal, we commend to Thy care astronauts Lousma and Fullerton as they orbit the earth . . . As the people of America follow the space journey and are united in their concern for its success, help us to be united in dedicated concern for peace on earth, for the relief of the poor, the oppressed, and the persecuted. We pray this in the name of the One whose mission is to 'gather in one all that are in heaven and on earth.' Amen."

RICHARD HALVERSON, CHAPLAIN OF THE UNITED STATES SENATE

For fourteen years, every day the United States Senate was in session, Richard Halverson offered a prayer as the Senate Chaplain. At times his prayers included names of senators who were ill or facing a special challenge. Sometimes his prayers encompassed national events, such as this one in 1982. Although he was known for establishing the bipartisan national prayer breakfasts, he seemed to value most his role as servant pastor to senators, their families and staff, and to government workers he met as he wandered Capitol Hill.

"You know, God, when life was easy, rolling merrily along, I didn't need You enough to shout. In fact it was kind of easy to forget You. Whispering was sufficient. But now life is tough; I'm stunned by its toughness, and I need You! Do You hear me now? I'm shouting!" [63]

BETH JAMESON

Her daughter, Kim, had never been sick a day in her life, so it was hard to believe the doctor's words, "I'm afraid it's leukemia." At first Beth Jameson hung on to the hope that between the intervention of God and modern medicine, her daughter would be healed. Finally reality settled down around her hope, and Beth found herself reaching for God's help as she had never done before. God did answer Beth's cry for help with the strength to encourage and comfort her daughter. The three years they had together until Kim's death were filled with mutual love and caring and a sharing of their deepening relationship with God.

"Lord, help Martha to be a bit more careful in her cooking!" [64]

ARNOLD PRATER

After a particularly difficult day, Arnold Prater came home to find the children ill, and his wife, Martha, exhausted after finishing all the washing and ironing. When she ruined their oven-cooked meal, Arnold felt there was room for improvement. In their usual prayer time together that evening, Arnold felt justified in talking to God about the situation. The result helped him to see the wisdom of what is now one of his rules for prayer: "Never try to manipulate, educate, direct, or accuse each other under the guise of prayer. Putting 'Dear God' in front of such words does not make them a prayer."

"Give us, O God, the vision which can see Thy love in the world in spite of human failure. Give us the faith to trust the goodness in spite of our ignorance and weakness. Give us the knowledge that we may continue to pray with understanding hearts, and show us what each one of us can do to set forward the coming of the day of universal peace. Amen."

FIRST PRAYER FROM SPACE

On Christmas Eve, 1968, the crew of Apollo 8 orbited the barren, pockmarked face of the moon, scouting the best place for a moon landing. This crew, Frank Borman, Bill Anders, and James Lovell, would not land, but would bring back critical information for those who would. As they watched the earth rise over the desolate wasteland of the moon—a sight no human eye had ever witnessed—they were struck with awe. Shortly after, the three men sent a message to earth. It was this prayer.

"Lord, I'm holding steady on to You,
and You'll have to see me through."

HARRIET TUBMAN

Known as "Moses" for leading more than 300 of her fellow slaves to freedom, Harriet Tubman prayed this prayer constantly. The danger of being captured by slave catchers and their dogs, the strain of moving frightened, and sometimes reticent, slaves on to safety, her precarious health—all of this only seemed to strengthen her resolve to complete the task she was sure had come from God.

"My Lord and my God, I have hoped in Thee,
O dearest Lord Jesus, deliver Thou me.
Bound by my chain,
In sorrow and pain,
I long sore for Thee.
Sighs and groans sending,
My knees to Thee bending,
I pray and beseech Thee,
Deliver Thou me." [65]

MARY, QUEEN OF SCOTS

Her cousin, Queen Elizabeth I, put Mary under house arrest when she came to England seeking her help. Because Mary was Catholic, Elizabeth was afraid to help her. Then when Mary and some of her friends hatched a plot to free her and overthrow Elizabeth, they were discovered. Under pressure, Elizabeth gave orders for Mary's beheading. Mary wrote this prayer before her execution, still hoping to be freed.

"O great and unsearchable God, who knowest my heart, and triest all my ways; with a humble dependence upon the support of Thy Holy Spirit, I yield myself up to Thee; as Thine own reasonable sacrifice, I return to Thee Thine own." [66]

CHARLES H. SPURGEON

Spurgeon was only eighteen in 1852 when he took on his first pastorate in a small Baptist church in London. Without formal theological training, he concentrated on the Old Testament stories and the New Testament Gospels. He preached with such fervor and humor that his congregation soon outgrew the building. For the next nine years the steady growth of his congregation made it necessary to move into a succession of larger buildings, until the Metropolitan Tabernacle was built to hold the crowd of 6,000 people eager to hear his messages.

". . . don't give up on me.
I can't make it without You." [67]

JOHNNY CASH

Johnny Cash had just spent a half hour on his knees, basking in the sweet presence of the Lord, and thanking Him for the miracle of pulling his life out of a hopeless rut. A sense of perfect peace settled over him as he climbed into bed. The years when addiction to drugs kept him enslaved were behind him. He knew now that he could make it—but only with the Lord's help.

"Here it is, God. You take it.
I can't handle it alone." [68]

PRESIDENT JIMMY CARTER

Jimmy Carter came into the Oval Office already knowing what it meant to trust God. He had found that God's love was a shield around him in the hard times. He knew that he could release his problems to God. Therefore, this prayer became his way of handling the unbelievable pressures of political life.

"Jesus, help me! I can lift my hand. I can do that much. You supply the feeling."[69]

CORRIE TEN BOOM

Corrie ten Boom recognized the man extending his hand as one of the most cruel of her Ravensbruck concentration camp guards. She had just preached a message about forgiveness to a Munich church group. Now this man told her that he had experienced God's forgiveness for the atrocities of Ravensbruck. Would *she* forgive him? It took all of Corrie's will to give him her hand as she prayed for help. And then the miracle happened. "This healing warmth seemed to flood my whole being," she said, "bringing tears to my eyes. 'I forgive you brother!' I cried. 'With all my heart.' "

"O Lord, reassure me with Your quickening Spirit; without You I can do nothing. Mortify in me all ambition, vanity, vainglory, worldliness, pride, selfishness, and resistance from God, and fill me with love, peace, and all the fruits of the Spirit. O Lord, I know not what I am, but to You I flee for refuge. I would surrender myself to You, trusting Your precious promises and against hope believing in hope. You are the same yesterday, today, and forever; and therefore, waiting on the Lord, I trust I shall at length renew my strength." [70]

WILLIAM WILBERFORCE

Five years after he was elected to the English Parliament in 1780, William Wilberforce had a conversion experience. As a result, his perspective on life changed. He began to push for more humane criminal laws and worked diligently to abolish the slave trade. The presence of the Lord in his life kept Wilberforce from giving up in discouragement, for it took Parliament more than twenty years to pass a bill abolishing the slave trade. Even then, it was not until a month after Wilberforce died that another bill passed that effectively halted this practice throughout the British Empire.

"O merciful God, consider my misery . . . give me grace . . . patiently to bear Thy works, assuredly knowing, that as Thou canst, so Thou wilt deliver me when it shall please Thee, nothing doubting or mistrusting Thy goodness towards me; for Thou knowest better what is good for me than I do." [71]

Lady Jane Grey

During the turbulent early 1500s in England, Lady Jane Grey, the fifteen-year-old granddaughter of Henry VII, was crowned queen. Her reign lasted only nine days, at which time Mary I's forces gathered strength and sent Lady Jane off to prison. Because of her youth, her life may have been spared, but her father joined a counter-rebellion. As a result, Lady Jane, her husband, and her father were all charged with treason and beheaded.

"With Your strength, please get us through this." [72]

STEVE BEDROSIAN

Atlanta Braves relief pitcher Steve Bedrosian pitched in the World Series and received the National League's coveted Cy Young Award. Then, in 1990, his young son, Cody, was diagnosed with leukemia, and Steve and his wife, Tammy, turned to God for strength. Soon after, Steve was traded to the Minnesota Twins and the Bedrosians discovered that the University of Minnesota had the best facility in the country for childhood leukemia. After years of chemotherapy and a bone marrow transplant, tests showed that Cody was in full remission. God has given the Bedrosians many opportunities to share their experiences and minister to others in crisis situations.

"Lord, just show me what's going on." [73]

CODY CUSTER

Sitting in the locker room just after a bullriding accident, World Champion Bull Rider Cody Custer questioned the wisdom of God in allowing an injury that would keep him from rodeo competition the rest of the season. But as he recuperated with his wife and three-month-old son back home in northern Arizona, Cody's faith was strengthened through regular fellowship with his church, and his son had time to get to know him as "Daddy." Now Cody sees the rodeo circuit as his mission field and helps produce rodeo schools for young people where he makes it clear that Jesus Christ, not the rodeo, makes a person a winner.

"Forget it, God. I can't keep going . . .
God, can You really change these kids?"[74]

Gladys Acuna

On Christmas Eve 1986, Gladys Acuna and Lisbeth Piedrasanta delivered a load of warm blankets to the filthy Guatemala City garbage dump—home to the city's poorest citizens. That was the beginning of an amazing ministry now called Casa del Alfarero (the potter's house), with a medical and dental clinic, food program, Bible teaching, and job training. Sometimes the hopelessness of the lives they serve—especially the children—makes them want to give up. But Gladys and Lisbeth refuse to be permanently discouraged and remain obedient to what they believe is God's call.

"Oh, please, dear Lord—show me the future." [75]

WALTER WANGERIN, JR.

It was not that Walt Wangerin had never prayed before about his growing affection for Thanne and what this might mean for the future. Home for the holidays, he knew he loved her and this was his last chance to ask her to marry him before returning to Oxford. If only he could see what marriage to Thanne would mean to them both. After his prayer he blurted, "Well, for heaven's sake, Thanne. Do you think that you should marry me?" Walter Wangerin is a Lutheran minister and a National Book Award winner. He is happily married to Thanne.

"Lord, make us masters of ourselves so that we can be servants of others. Take our minds and think through them, take our lips and speak through them, take our hearts and set them afire."[76]

ANONYMOUS

George Gallup collects prayers. This is one of his favorites. The famous pollster also creates his own prayers, for prayer is an integral part of his life. "It suggests to me an ongoing sense of the presence of God, which is the ultimate goal in developing prayer."

"Give me a pure heart—that I may see Thee,
A humble heart—that I may hear Thee,
A heart of love—that I may serve Thee,
A heart of faith—that I may abide in Thee."[77]

DAG HAMMARSKJOLD

This prayer was found in Dag Hammarskjold's diary after he was killed in a plane crash in 1961 on a United Nations mission to the Congo. With his quiet diplomacy, Hammarskjold expanded the influence of the UN. His diary documented the ongoing and significant relationship with God which formed the underpinnings of his life.

"Thou hast giv'n so much to me,
Give one thing more, a grateful heart." [78]

GEORGE HERBERT

From early in his life, George Herbert wanted to become a clergyman. Born in 1593 to privilege and nobility, he graduated from Cambridge. Then an appointment as public orator kept him from the ministry until only three years before his death. Herbert's devotional poetry, simple and intimate, won him a place in literary history following his death.

"Thou hast made me, And shall Thy worke decay?
Repaire me now, for now mine end doth haste,
I runne to death, and death meets me as fast,
And all my pleasures are like yesterday . . .
But our old subtle foe so tempteth me,
That not one houre my selfe I can sustaine,
Thy Grace may wing me to prevent his art,
And Thou like Adamant draw mine iron heart."

JOHN DONNE

Sixteen years before his death in 1631, the poet, John Donne, was ordained a clergyman. Donne contended, as did his "hero" St. Augustine, with the problems of flesh versus spirit. Much of his writing, and especially his prayers, reflect this constant battle. Donne was considered one of the most eloquent preachers of his day, but his words live on in his poetry.

"Father in heaven, You who have forgiven man in the past, forgive these men also. Do not let them perish in their sins but bring them into Yourself." [79]

KEFA SEMPANGI

Easter morning 1973, Kampala, Uganda. Pastor Kefa Sempangi had just led over 7,000 people in worship. Now five of Idi Amin's hit men waited for him. "We are going to kill you," the leader announced. "If you have something to say, say it before you die." Almost fainting, Sempangi answered, "My life is dead and hidden in Christ, I will pray to God that after you have killed me, He will spare you from eternal destruction." Instead of shooting, the leader said, "Will you pray for us now?" After Sempangi's prayer, the five men left the church. Later, the leader, a man who had tortured and killed more than 200 people, found forgiveness and new life in Christ.

"Lord, have mercy on me . . . To Christ
I commend my soul; Jesu receive my soul." [80]

QUEEN ANNE OF BOLEYN

Anne Boleyn had been married to King Henry VIII of England only three years when she was caught in the middle of a faction in the Tudor court and charged with high treason. King Henry sent her to the Tower of London with her brother, Lord Rochford, who was also implicated, and ordered the beheading of them both. She was known for her care for the poor and her deep Christian faith.

"O Lord, great distress has come upon me; my cares threaten to crush me, and I do not know what to do. O God, be gracious to me and help me. Give me strength to bear what You send, and do not let fear rule over me. Take a father's care of my wife and children . . . whether I live or die, I am with You, and You, my God, are with me. Lord, I wait for Your salvation and for Your kingdom. Amen." [81]

DIETRICH BONHOEFFER

In 1943, German pastor and theologian, Dietrich Bonhoeffer, wrote this prayer for his fellow prisoners in a concentration camp. At the beginning of World War II, Bonhoeffer turned down sanctuary in America to stand with his countrymen against the Third Reich. As a member of the inner circle of the resistance movement, Bonhoeffer was able to relay important information and escort groups of Jews to safety outside Germany. As a result of his activities, he endured torture, weeks in solitary confinement, and eventually was executed by the Nazis at Flossenburg concentration camp at dawn on April 9, 1945.

"Lord, protect me."[82]

Jeb Magruder

The night before Jeb Magruder was to be transferred to the Holabird facility where Herb Kalmbach and Chuck Colson, also indicted in Watergate, were interned, a fellow prisoner warned him of a plan to "get Magruder." God protected Magruder, and after seven months in prison, he was released. Following a time with Young Life Campaign as their Director of Communications, Magruder went on to seminary and a degree in Divinity and Social Work.

"Although within us there are wounds, Lord Christ, above all there is the miracle of Your mysterious presence. Thus, made lighter or even set free, we are going with You, the Christ, from one discovery to another." [83]

ROGER SCHUTZ

In 1940, twenty-five-year-old Roger Schutz moved to a house in the village of Taize in southeast France. His dream was to gather together a community of people with the same burning desire he had to follow Jesus Christ joyfully and obediently. Soon his house became a shelter for Jews and other refugees of World War II, and he was joined by others who shared his dream. Today the Taize retreat center attracts visitors from all over the world, from all Christian traditions.

"Lord, I believe You're in this revival meeting. People's being saved. I don't have any medicine and if You want me to preach, heal me now." [84]

Rev. Ben Cook

Rev. Ben Cook pastored more than twenty churches in the mountains of North Carolina before he died in 1979. During a successful revival at a Southern Baptist church where he was preaching, he became very ill just before the evening service. No one else could take his place. Rev. Cook walked across the little creek near the church and prayed for help. "The Lord healed me that minute," he said, and he went back to preach the evening service.

"Lord, I'll take Your Word and I'll go and stand by as long as life lasts by your help."[85]

REV. BLY OWENS

Walking the railroad track that ran through the Appalachian Mountains, Bly Owens had a miraculous vision of Jesus Christ that changed his life. But he was willing to do just about anything except become a preacher. One night as he lay gravely ill with blood poisoning from a rotting wisdom tooth, he heard God say, "Bly, go into the world and warn people of the great wrath of God." Three hours later, after his prayer of assent, he began to heal.

"... We only ask You to help us to teach these people so they won't spend all of the future in the big fire."[86]

Tadyawan Tribe Believer

When Caroline Stickley and her partner, Dode Pack, trekked into the Mindoro mountains to bring the Gospel to the primitive Tadyawan tribe, they trusted God with the results. Years later, they sat in a raised-pole hut on this Philippine island, surrounded by Tadyawan Christians who had not only believed the message for themselves, but were now reaching out to other villages—even other tribes—with the Good News.

"Oh Heavenly Father, Your plans are always so much bigger than ours." [87]

Romulo Saune

Romulo Saune's heart was full of gratitude after attending a gathering of Quechua Indian Christians. Since becoming a Christian as a young man, Romulo had committed his life to translating the Bible for his people. His work had a sense of urgency, since he knew he was targeted by the Shining Path, a powerful Communist terrorist group with connections to the drug cartel. When Shining Path guerrillas finally gunned him down on a road, Romulo left a completed Quechua translation of the Bible and countless Quechua souls ready to meet God because of their faith in Jesus Christ.

"Great God, we are Your people—how we struggle to make that real! We are people with feelings—but we repress and deny them, misuse and misdirect them. We are people of strength—but we work for just "things," drain our energy on ourselves . . . We are people who can communicate—but we speak too harshly and thoughtlessly, hold back what is upbuilding and needed. We are people of Your Spirit—but we blunt Your penetrating power, and squelch Your renewing moves. Struggle with us, our God, now and in daily ways. Amen." [88]

People of LaSalle Street Church

In the fall of 1961, when Bill Leslie preached his first sermon at what was then known as Elm-LaSalle Church in Chicago, he felt confident of what he could do with this branch of the venerable Moody Church. But he didn't realize the power of a group of Christians willing to meet head on the challenge of poverty, prejudice, and violence in an inner-city neighborhood. LaSalle Street Church spawned a counseling center, a tutoring program for the youth of the notorious Cabrini Green housing project, a legal aid clinic, and united churches in the area to build multi-racial/economic housing to help bring stability to the area.

"Our Father, help us feel Thy presence, for otherwise our being here is nothing. . . . Here is the work of our hands. Take it for Thy use. We would see Thy glory as it enfolds this house and makes of it a House of God. . . O Lord. May the silence of these woods and good fields hush the clamant voices of our sins. Work Thou a work in our souls, Creator, mighty and complete." [89]

DAYSPRING COMMUNITY GROUP

In the late 1970s, a group of Christians from the Church of the Savior in Washington, D.C. watched a dream come true as they dedicated the lodge they had built at their Dayspring farm retreat. Since then Dayspring has given hospitality to groups of underprivileged children, burned-out adults, and men and women needing a place to pursue a renewed commitment to God.

"God, give them courage for my dressing changes, even when I flinch with pain." [90]

MYRA LOU BARNARD

Friday nights, when she was taken to surgery for the painful debridement and changes of the dressing on her burns, Myra Lou was aware that this was also a painful process for her nurses. They were her friends—fellow Wycliffe missionaries who had also come to the Philippines to translate the Bible into tribal languages. When Myra Lou was burned over most of her body in a kerosene refrigerator explosion, these women worked around the clock to tend to her needs as she slowly healed.

"Blessed are You, Lord of All Gifts,
for Your masterful handiwork: the nose.
I thank You for the gift of my nose
and its marvelous power of smelling life . . .
Show to me, Lord,
how my nose can be a source of my prayer
as I awaken to, sense, and enjoy
the ten thousand different incenses
That arise from all things in praise of You,
their holy and artistic Creator." [91]

EDWARD HAYS

From his seven years as pastor of a group of Pottawatomie Indians in Kansas, Edward Hays developed a new awareness of the wonders of God's creation—including such taken-for-granted creative works as the nose.

"God, thank You tonight for being with me, thank You for life, for the power of the Holy Spirit that enables us to carry out this wonderfully insane new order of living. Please give me the power to be a peacemaker. I've got a long way to go, and please help me to stay out of step and out of tune with the world's way of doing things." [92]

Bill Milliken

Walking home through the troubled streets of New York City's Lower East Side, Bill Milliken thought about the meeting of young Latin revolutionaries he'd met with tonight and their reaction to the words he'd read from "Chairman Jesus." No wonder they couldn't "buy it." Chairman Mao advocated revolution through violence. Jesus' radical revolution would come through love—but a tough love that could transform the despair and violence of these streets into hope and peace.

"Lord Jesus, obedient Son of God,
we come as disobedient children.
Charged with responsibility for a beautiful, bountiful garden, we have acted as immoral and greedy absentee landlords, disregarding its needs. . . .
Instead of obediently dressing and keeping our garden, we are madly undressing and destroying it.
We've come together here today to repent.
Lord Jesus, born in a manger, simplify our needs, purify our desires.
Help us become obedient children
of our Heavenly Father. Amen."

COREAN BAKKE

This prayer was written for an ecumenical service for the environment in October of 1993. Corean Bakke is an artist/author/musician who was responsible for the music of the 1989 Lausanne Conference on Evangelism in Manila. Hoping to equally represent the different peoples of the world, Bakke spent months contacting musicians from remote areas of the globe, researching their music, and compiling a hymnal that included music of many nations in praise and commitment to one Lord Jesus Christ.

"How is it, my God, that You have given me this hectic busy life when I have so little time to enjoy Your presence. Throughout the day people are waiting to speak to me and even at meals I have to continue talking to people about their needs and problems. . . . I know that You are constantly beside me, yet I am usually so busy that I ignore You. If You want me to remain so busy, please force me to think about and love You even in the midst of such hectic activity. If You do not want me so busy, please release me from it, showing how others can take over my responsibilities." [93]

TERESA OF AVILA

A product of the Carmelite spirituality of the 1500s, Teresa's devotion to Christ blew hot and cold until her 40s. Then a series of mystical experiences with the Lord solidified her faith. She helped John of the Cross found a new order of Carmelites and worked untiringly in administration of the order. Her honest and practical prayers demonstrate the close relationship she enjoyed with God.

"Lord, Satan tells me that neither Thy mercy, nor Christ's blood is sufficient to save my soul; Lord, shall I honour Thee most, by believing Thou wilt, and canst? or him, by believing that Thou neither wilt, nor canst? Lord, I would fain honour Thee, by believing that Thou wilt, and canst." [94]

JOHN BUNYAN

In his famous *Pilgrim's Progress,* John Bunyan's view of life as a journey full of dangers, pitfalls, and conflict between good and evil is well illustrated. Although he was sure of the goodness and power of God, Bunyan spent much of his life agonizing over his own sinfulness, at last coming to a glorious assurance of his salvation through Christ.

"God, if You don't save me now, I'm going to die. I've done everything I know how to do and I don't know anything else to do."[95]

GRANNY (ROSIE) REED

As a twelve-year-old girl in Appalachia, Rosie Reed hadn't thought much about her soul until her father challenged her to do so. After a serious discussion with her cousin, Zadie, Rosie decided she'd better go to the altar at the next church meeting. She and Zodie answered every altar call without any visible results until, during one meeting, Zodie jumped up and said, "Oh, I'm saved, and God's going to save you." After Rosie's desperate prayer, she was finally released from doubt and could celebrate her salvation with Zodie. Granny Reed lived for the Lord into her nineties.

"Heavenly Father, Thou hast taken Papa to be with Thyself, and in Thy holy Word Thou hast promised to take care of mother, brother, sisters, and myself. When I say or do anything to grieve Thee, may I quickly confess to Thee and so keep happy and smiling for Thee. Amen." [96]

Lawrence Crabb, Sr.

The great flu epidemic of 1917 took Lawrence Crabb's father, leaving his mother with four children to raise. The influence and nurturing of his Christian parents was evident in young Crabb's prayer following his father's death. Lawrence Crabb grew up to raise his own family as a Christian father. His son, Dr. Larry Crabb, Jr., founder and director of the Institute of Biblical Counseling says, "Dad always used the *King James English* when he prayed. But it never sounded artificial or strained . . . I got the idea that, to him, God was a real person, too big to figure out but available enough to be known."

"Dear God, please forgive me all the sins I have ever done and all the sins I ever will be doing. And please forgive everyone else all the sins they have ever done and all the sins they ever will be doing."

ROLF TANGVALD, AGE 9

According to his mother, author Christine Tangvald, young Rolf seemed to believe that this often repeated prayer should just about cover the whole situation. Today Rolf is an assistant states attorney in Spokane, Washington, and listens to the prayers of his own three children.

"I am sure You will forgive this wretched Pranzini. I shall believe You have done so even if he does not confess or give any other sign of repentance, for I have complete faith in the infinite mercy of Jesus. But I ask You for just one sign of his repentance to encourage me."[97]

THERESE OF LISIEUX

This prayer of the beloved nineteenth century nun is an example of the burden she felt for lost souls. When she heard of a murderer who had been condemned to death, she began to pray fervently for his soul. Her request for "just one sign of his repentance," was answered when she read in a newspaper that Pranzini had reached for a crucifix and kissed it just before he was beheaded.

"Dear God," I prayed, all unafraid
(as girls are wont to be),
"I do not want a handsome man—
but let him be like Thee.
And let his face have character,
a ruggedness of soul.
And let his whole life show, dear God,
a singleness of goal.
And when he comes,
as he will come, with quiet eyes aglow—
I'll understand that he's the man
I prayed for long ago." [98]

RUTH BELL GRAHAM

That Ruth Bell had deliberately committed the matter of a lifemate into the hands of the Lord, is evident in this prayer she prayed during her student days at Wheaton College. While there, she gained a reputation for her devout prayer life. Every morning she was awake by 5 A.M. to spend two hours in prayer and Bible reading. After showing a copy of this prayer to Stanley High, the author of *Billy Graham,* Ruth is said to have asked, "Do you wonder that I believe in answered prayer?"

"Yes, Lord . . . This is why You've put me here. For doors to open; for Your sweet, strong, and holy voice to be heard throughout the land."[99]

LAUREN HOMER

While visiting a new church in Kazakhstan, southeast of Russia, Lauren Homer thanked the Lord for a story she heard of God's moving in lives parched for His love: A group of Christians sang hymns after sharing dessert in a church member's apartment. Soon, one by one, apartment doors all over the building opened to the sound of these songs of witness and praise. Lauren began visiting Russia when, restless and bored with her life as a Washington, D.C. lawyer, she felt a nudging to do what she could in the corrupt Russian legal system.

"God, I believe (or rather, I must believe or despair)—help Thou my unbelief. Take away my heart of stone and give me a heart of flesh."[100]

DOROTHY DAY

Ironically, it was through the influence of a man who was both an anarchist and an atheist that Dorothy Day found God. She had never known a companionship like the one she shared with Forster Batterham. But the more she was drawn toward God, the more Dorothy knew the day would come when she would have to choose between Forster and God. She chose God. Dorothy Day's passion for justice and her compassion for the poor led her to cofound the Catholic Worker movement. At seventy-five, she was given an award by Notre Dame University for "comforting the afflicted and afflicting the comfortable, virtually all her life."

"Now, Lord, if there is mercy for me, let me find it." [101]

PETER CARTWRIGHT

A circuit-riding Methodist preacher of the early 1800s, Peter Cartwright was vocal in his opposition to slavery. In 1832 he defeated Abraham Lincoln for a seat in the Illinois legislature, but was defeated by Lincoln in the 1846 election. As a teenager, Cartwright had already enjoyed the drinking, gambling, horse racing, and dancing of frontier life. But his devout mother's prayers followed him. At sixteen he was converted after months of anguish over his soul.

"Lord Jesus Christ, Son of God, have mercy on me, a sinner." [102]

THE DESERT FATHERS

This simple, but powerful, prayer has become known as the "Jesus Prayer." It was first used by Christians in the third and fourth centuries who believed that the best way to be truly committed to Jesus Christ was to go off to the Egyptian desert in solitude and prayer. There they would live in isolated austerity, reciting the Psalms, interspersed with the Jesus Prayer. Because the prayer evoked the name of the One before whom demons tremble, it became a tool in their ongoing battle with the demons they believed inhabited the desert.

"Dear God, these are anxious times. . . . Alas, there doesn't seem to be much You Yourself can do about our circumstances, about our lives. Neither do I hold You responsible . . . but we must . . . defend Your dwelling place inside us to the last. . . . There are those who want to put their bodies in safe keeping but who are nothing more now than a shelter for a thousand fears and bitter feelings. And then they say, "I shan't let them get me into their clutches." But they forget that no one is in their clutches who is in Your arms." [103]

ETTY HILLESUM

During the height of the persecution of Jews in Holland during World War II, a Dutch Jewish woman hung on to her faith in God. Etty Hillesum lived in Amsterdam during the Nazi occupation and was then sent to Auschwitz. When she knew she was about to be exterminated, she gave her diary to a friend who later had it published as *An Interrupted Life.*

"God . . . Where were You in Vietnam?"
An ex-Marine

"Lord, You have delivered us from the scourge of war. May we who have been scarred by war be reconciled to each other, to our enemies, and to You. May we become peacemakers in all that we do. . . . Grant to those who are yet untouched by war the great gift of continued freedom from the terrible agonies of armed conflict. We ask this through Jesus Christ, Your Son, our Lord. Amen." [104]

PRAYER OF RECONCILIATION

The desperately shouted prayer of an ex-Marine echoes the feelings of many whose memories are scarred with unwanted sights and sounds and feelings from the conflict in Vietnam. After three years in Vietnam, Chaplain William Mahedy came home to work with the veterans of that conflict and help them readjust. Ten years after the Vietnam War ended, Mahedy helped lead a retreat in Santa Barbara, California for reconciliation and healing of the wounds of that war.

"Grant us prudence in proportion to our power, wisdom in proportion to our science, humaneness in proportion to our wealth and might."

THOMAS MERTON

On April 12, 1962, during Holy Week, a prayer for peace by Thomas Merton was read in the United States House of Representatives by a Connecticut congressman. As a Trappist monk, Merton had hoped for solitude at the Abbey of Gethsemani in Kentucky, but his writings advocating the abolition of war and the settling of international disputes by nonviolent means thrust him into the public eye. Later, the abbot general of his monastic order issued a directive that Merton publish no more on the subjects of war and peace.

"We Praise Thee, O God; we acknowledge Thee to be the Lord. All the earth doth worship Thee, the Father Everlasting . . . O Lord, in Thee have I trusted." [105]

Christians from Rangoon

After the liberation of Burma in 1944, a group of Christians from Rangoon visited the communal grave of four women teachers and four schoolgirls killed by a band of Japanese sympathizers. When the band routed out Christians who were Karen by birth, the headmistress of the school could not keep silent. "We are not Karens," she said, "but we are Christians and we must stand by them." The little group prayed together, then went out and faced death. As the Rangoon Christians stood by the martyrs' grave, they sang the traditional *Te Deum*—a prayer of thanksgiving for these brave sisters in Christ.

"May our home be made holy, O God, by Your light. May the light of love and truth shine upon us all as a blessing from You. May our table and our family be consecrated by Your Divine Presence at this meal and at all our family meals. Amen."[106]

JEWISH FAMILY PRAYER

As the Jewish Sabbath begins at sundown each Friday, this prayer is recited by the mother of the house, or by a married daughter. At the same time, the Sabbath candles are lit.

"Oh, Father God, tho' I have missed the heights
To which I yearn to go in ways of right,
I cannot yield to bleak despondency.
I must not, since Your Love still follows me.
I'm young no more; my feet are tired and slow.
They want to linger when I long to go.
Please, Father God, is it patience that I need?
Should I cease fretting? Help me, Lord, I plead,
That at the ending of each granted day
That You would let me have, I'll humbly pray,
Not for swift feet, but for a heart content
To go on slowly 'til my days are spent . . ."

DAISY LENORE BILBY

Daisy Bilby penned this prayer on her eightieth birthday in 1961. The prayer reflects the optimistic faith that characterized her life. When she was twenty and teaching in a one-room school, she lost her heart to a young Methodist minister. For fifty-five years she and her husband served churches in the Midwest and produced seven children. At ninety-two, Daisy Lenore Bilby went to be with her Lord.

"Lord, if You'll forgive me for marrying him, I'll never do it again." [107]

RUTH BELL GRAHAM

Very early in their marriage, a disappointment drove Ruth Graham to pray what she calls, "The dumbest prayer I ever prayed." Billy decided to go with some visiting bachelor friends into the city for the day. Ruth needed respite from the four walls of their apartment and asked to come along. But Billy made it clear it was a "guys only" trip. After the men drove away, doubts about this man she'd married were followed by Ruth's tearful prayer. Billy did realize his insensitivity and received forgiveness.

"O God, You ordained marriage for Your children and gave us the creative ability to love others. In this sacred moment, we present these two precious people to You. O God, give Woody and Andrea the ability to keep the covenant they have made. When selfishness shows itself, grant generosity; when misunderstanding intrudes, give patience and gentleness. When times of trouble and stress come, give them a strong faith and abiding hope. Make their home a shelter from that which destroys and a school where they may be fitted for Your kingdom."

WEDDING PRAYER

This was the prayer of dedication at the 1986 wedding of Andrea Tanner and Woody Bakke.

"Dear God, show me what is the matter!" [108]

KEITH MILLER

In the beginning the adventure of becoming a Christian flooded Keith Miller's spirit with joy. "But after a while," he says, "there came an uneasiness in my inner life. I realized something was wrong in my relationship with God. . . ." He asked for direction, and God put His finger on the problem: sin that he had repressed needed confessing. Miller confessed to God, but it was not until he found a trusted friend to confess to that he experienced release and a deepening of his relationship with God—and with his friend.

"Lord, I take Thee at Thy word. Now Thou knowest that I do search for Thee with all my heart, and that I have come here to pray to Thee; and Thou hast promised to hear me." [109]

CHARLES G. FINNEY

The great evangelist, Charles Finney, found himself faced with the message of salvation when, as a young lawyer, he studied Mosaic Law. This delving into Scripture brought the rest of the Bible to his attention, and he came to realize that God was asking for more than intellectual assent to the words of Scripture.

"My Jesus, my King, my life, my all; I again dedicate my whole self to Thee. Accept me and grant, O gracious Father, that ere this year is gone I may finish my task. In Jesus' name I ask it. Amen, so let it be." [110]

DAVID LIVINGSTONE

In Africa, on his fifty-ninth birthday, David Livingstone made this entry in his diary. A year later he was found dead, in a kneeling position, beside his bed. For more than thirty years Livingstone explored and evangelized Africa, traveling all through central and southern Africa from coast to coast. God used him not only in the evangelization of Africa, but also to bring the horrors of the African slave trade to the attention of both Great Britain and America.

"Oh God, if You want our little girl with You in heaven, then You take her, because I know I'm going to see her again, be with her again, for all eternity. So if You have to, God, just take her. But Lord . . . I really do want her back." [111]

IKE KEAY

Exhausted from their work at a Christian children's home, Ike and Carolyn Keay needed this lazy day on a North Carolina lake. Suddenly their two-year-old daughter, Debbie, fell overboard. Frantic, Ike dived in and for long minutes searched underwater for his tiny daughter. He'd already used up precious time when he sensed God urging him to try another spot near the boat. Deep down in the black water his hand felt Debbie's head, and he quickly pulled her to the surface, knowing she would be unconscious by now. Miraculously, Debbie's eyes were open and her mouth was clamped shut. The Keays realized that God shut her mouth and kept her from drowning.

"Please, don't let anything terrible happen. Please." [112]

MADELEINE L'ENGLE

When Madeleine L'Engle was a child, she and her parents spent a summer at the beach with her beloved grandmother. Madeleine called her "Dearma." One night that summer, as she prepared for bed, Madeleine felt a sense of foreboding. With childlike faith she prayed for help. The answer to her prayer was a certainty that Dearma would die that night. Before daylight Madeleine woke her parents. When they looked in on Dearma, they found her breathing her last breaths.

"For this new morning and its light, For rest and shelter of the night, For health and strength, for love and friends, For everything Thy goodness sends, We thank Thee, Heavenly Father. In Jesus' name, Amen."

THE THIESSEN FAMILY

This prayer launched Sunday mornings for the Thiessen family as they held hands around the breakfast table. Next came the traditional cold cereal with bananas or fresh fruit and mother's freshly baked streusel coffee cake. The scene repeated "every Sunday morning as long as I remember, growing up," author Neta Thiessen Jackson recalls.

"Dear Jesus, please help Mommy sew her hair back on."

BONNI RODRIGUEZ, AGE 3

Three year-old Bonni found great comfort in holding and twisting her mommy's beautiful waist-length hair. She seemed to treasure it in the same way other children treasure a blanket—a security blanket. Early on, Bonni's parents had begun teaching her that she could talk to Jesus about anything. So, when her mother cut her hair to shoulder length, Bonni went to Jesus with her problem.

"O Lord, I am just like a little child when it comes to spiritual knowing; what is it You have to teach me today?" [113]

Karen Burton Mains

Her overfull days of constant cleaning, cooking, and nurturing of children, husband, and inner-city congregation could not stifle the growing desire for a fresh taste of God. Karen Mains' prayer became a daily plea that gradually opened new places in her heart. She found that when she stopped talking and began listening to God, she could hear. In her book, *Karen! Karen!* Mains writes, "He taught me that it was Himself I wanted and needed and desired, not my intellectual pursuits, not the cuddling of this good world, not even myself. It was He I wanted and none other."

"The Lord bless you and keep you: The Lord make His face to shine upon you and be gracious unto you: the Lord life up His countenance upon you and give you peace."

NUMBERS 6:24-26

This graceful blessing is heard as the benediction of many Christian church services. It was also the blessing given to the people by the high priest in the ancient temple, and is still used in Jewish services today. Some rabbis sing this blessing with their face covered by a prayer shawl called a "tallit."

"O God, I don't pray enough. Forgive my lack of prayer—my personal prayer, prayer with my family, prayer for my church. O God, forgive me!" [114]

Pastor at Conference

One pastor responded with this prayer when Evelyn Christenson spoke to a group of ministers and challenged them with a statement by Dr. Paul Yonggi Cho, pastor of a one-million member church in Seoul, Korea. How did his church grow to that incredible size? "Americans stay after church and eat," he said. "We stay after church and pray."

". . . for unity among the staff, that they come with renewed zeal to work together . . . for unity among the students . . . for the incoming freshman. Please still their fears . . . for racial unity, that they can find a bond and be friends . . . for students to have an eagerness to learn, to work hard on their classes." [115]

"Moms in Touch"

At their weekly hour-long meetings, 30,000 groups of "Moms in Touch" across the United States and in some foreign countries do nothing but pray for their kids and their schools. Since 1984, when Fern Nichols, concerned about her junior high sons, asked another mother to pray with her, Moms in Touch groups have formed to support their kids through the public school experience. These prayer excerpts came from a group of Illinois Moms praying for their sons and daughters at the beginning of a new school year.

"Lord, I can't. There is just no way I can go talk to those ladies when I don't know the first thing about serenity!"[116]

GIGI GRAHAM TCHIVIDJIAN

The serenity of a month of vacation in the mountains evaporated quickly for Gigi Tchividjian. A series of crises beginning with her grandmother's death, and including a hurricane and then her mother's surgery, compounded the usual hassle of managing a household with seven children. When it was time to pack for a speaking engagement in which she'd be addressing 4,000 women on the subject of *serenity,* Gigi felt more than inadequate. But as she prayed, God made it clear to her that He would honor her earlier prayers about sharing *His* message alone—and God had something to say on the subject of serenity.

"Lord . . . let my faith grow again. Let it be strong. If I suffer, let it be for a reason—because I love You and do Your will. Let my newfound zeal outmatch their contempt for You." [117]

REINHOLD KERSTAN

Reinhold Kerstan had no choice, nor did his pastor father. Too young for Hitler's army, at thirteen he was sent off to a Hitler Youth camp for indoctrination and training. At the camp the other boys knew his father was a pastor and teased him mercilessly. One day they stripped him, slapped him, and tied him to a bunk bed. It was the jolt Reinhold needed to jump-start his commitment to Christ. God rewarded his faithful witness in the months following as, one-by-one, some of these same boys gave their lives to Jesus Christ.

"Lead, Kindly Light, amidst
the encircling gloom,
Lead Thou me on;
The night is dark, and I am far from home;
Lead Thou me on;
Keep Thou my feet; I do not ask to see
The distant scene—one step enough for me."

John Henry Newman

Though quiet, scholarly, and not a seeker of the limelight, John Henry Newman became a leader of a renewal movement in the Anglican church in nineteenth century England. Newman saw the church becoming liberal and lifeless and many agreed with him and supported his movement. But the struggle was painful—spiritually and emotionally. Newman's famous prayer hymn attests to that struggle.

"If You can do anything with this life, Jesus, go ahead and do it. I'm messed up. I don't have no place to go. I hate my father. I hate my mother. I even hate myself. Please, for God's sake, if there's anything You can do, do it!"[118]

NEW YORK CITY TEENAGER

Bill Milliken overheard this prayer when he walked into a dark cabin at the end of another discouraging day at Young Life's Frontier camp. It came from one of the defiant New York inner city teenagers he had driven across country to attend the camp. Milliken had hoped to return with the born-again nucleus of a Young Life club but since they'd arrived there had been no indication that anything was getting through to these kids. Thank God, here was the beginning.

"Naked I wait Thy love's uplifted stroke!
My harness piece by piece Thou hast hewn from me,
And smitten me to my knee;
I am defenseless utterly."[119]

FRANCIS THOMPSON

This prayer from Francis Thompson's famous poem, *The Hound of Heaven,* illustrates both his despair and his eventual surrender to God who pursued him. Thompson was a romantic dreamer who fought an addiction to opium for much of his life.

"Today—one which I've never lived before and one which I will never get to live again. Thank You, Lord, for this incredible gift. The surprise of unwrapping it holds wonder and the privilege of excitement." [120]

Tim Hansel

At a time in his life when he realized he must choose between society's standards of "success" and truly living, Tim Hansel decided to truly live. He began to consciously relish time rather than hurry from one experience or task to another, to enjoy silence instead of filling his moments with sound and activity. He began to see each day as a unique gift from the Lord.

"Thou, Lord, makest a fruitful field a barren wilderness and a barren wilderness a fruitful field; Thou bringest down and settest up; Thou killest and makest alive; all honour and glory be to Thee, O Lord of glory!" [121]

George Fox

In the midst of the religious turmoil of seventeenth century England, George Fox and his followers established a religious movement that held to the priesthood of all believers, continuing personal revelation by the Inner Light of Christ, and concern for the oppressed. Because of his strong commitment to what he perceived as true Christianity, Fox suffered persecution and imprisonment.

"Lord, God, forgive me . . . for my hatred." [122]

ELIZABETH MORRIS

Their only child was killed by a drunken driver at age eighteen. For almost two years Elizabeth and Frank Morris could feel nothing but hatred for Tommy Pigage, the young man who caused their son's death. They pushed for the death penalty. But God could not let this Christian couple be consumed by revenge, and a miracle of forgiveness happened—first with Elizabeth and then with Frank. Through their forgiveness, Tommy Pigage became a Christian and his ten-year prison sentence was revoked.

"Oh, Love, can it be that You have called me with such love and made me to know in one instant that which tongue cannot utter?"[123]

Catherine of Genoa

In 1473, depressed with her arranged marriage to an unfaithful gambling husband, Catherine Adorno recited her sins to her confessor as usual. This time she experienced not only a deep awareness of her own spiritual need, but an overwhelming sense of the love of God. She left the church, changed forever, her depression lifted. Her response to this "mountaintop experience" was to live out her life in service to the poor and sick of Genoa. A few months later, her husband also experienced a conversion, and joined her in her work.

"Oh God, I pray that this violence that can be seen coming may not be hastened, since the left and the popular political groups see no other way for the country's genuine transformation."[124]

Archbishop Oscar Romero of El Salvador

During his last weeks of life, Archbishop Romero continued to pray for and work toward an alternative solution to civil war in El Salvador. At the Basilica of the Sacred Heart in San Salvador his homilies were full of words from the Gospels against violence, calling the people to courage in the face of injustice. On Monday, March 24, 1980, Romero was gunned down as he celebrated the Eucharist at the funeral for a friend's mother. On Wednesday, 5,000 mourners accompanied his body through the streets of San Salvador in final tribute to their spiritual leader.

"It would be comforting to be able to say . . . to You, 'Lord!' and confidently await Your command. Comforting—but alas, it would not be true. The one thing above all others that You require of us is, surely, the truth. I have to confess, then, that I see only fitfully. . . . And You? A living person in the world . . . at the intersection of time and eternity—nailed there—You confront us . . . You have overcome history. You came as light into the world in order that whoever believed in You should not remain in darkness. Your light shines in the darkness, and the darkness has not overcome it. Nor ever will." [125]

MALCOLM MUGGERIDGE

British journalist Malcolm Muggeridge wrestled from childhood with the meaning of life, and belief in the existence of God. He was put off by what he observed in both the church and in society. It was while he was on assignment in the Soviet Union that he felt most drawn to Jesus Christ. In an Easter service in Kiev he watched the "gray, hungry faces . . . how they sang—about how there was no help except in You . . ." At age sixty-six, Muggeridge wrote the above prayer in *Jesus Rediscovered,* a book about his faith journey.

"Oh God, honor all these folks coming together and bring peace to Bosnia."[126]

People of First Baptist Church, Fairborn, Ohio

During the twenty-one days of negotiations in Dayton, Ohio to find a way to end the conflict between Bosnia, Serbia, and Croatia, God's people all over the world prayed. When negotiations were at a critical point, First Baptist Church members held a time of prayer following their Sunday service. On November 21st the peace accord was signed, a hopeful ending, according to the *New York Times,* of "nearly four years of terror and ethnic bloodletting that have left a quarter of a million people dead in the worst war in Europe since World War II."

"God, if You ever helped mortal man, help me to get that ball, and You haven't very much time to make up Your mind, either." [127]

BILLY SUNDAY

Shortly after Billy Sunday gave his life to Jesus Christ at Pacific Garden Mission in Chicago, he and his fellow White Sox players went up against Detroit. The game was tense, for the winners would claim the championship. When a Detroit player batted the ball high over the outfield, Billy knew this would be the deciding play. He caught the ball, but was almost trampled by a team of horses as he rolled with it off the edge of the field. Billy Sunday went from baseball fame to become one of America's most effective evangelists.

"Lord, whose spirit is so good and so gentle in all things, and who art so compassionate that not only all prosperity but even all afflictions that come to Thine elect are the results of Thy compassion: grant me grace that I may not do as the pagans do in the condition to which Thy justice has reduced me; grant that as a true Christian I may recognize Thee as my Father and as my God, in whatever estate I find myself, since the change in my condition brings no change in Thine own. . . . Grant then, Lord, that I may conform to Thy will, just as I am, that being sick as I am, I may glorify Thee in my sufferings." [128]

BLAISE PASCAL

In poor health for most of his life, French scientist and religious philosopher Blaise Pascal found hope and consolation in his deep Christian faith. When he knew that his illness would soon result in death, Pascal wrote this beautiful prayer, asking God to use the illness for His glory.

"We kneel before You right now on this broadcast and we pray for men like John Warner. And we pray for Ronald Reagan and we pray for his cabinet and we pray for the leaders of our nation. O God, may the members of Congress turn from partisanship and may they turn to the Lord today. And may they know that, O God, the situation is much more critical than we'd like to think. . . . Thank You, Father, we believe . . . that You will come and bring righteousness to this land." [129]

PAT ROBERTSON

Following an interview on the "700 Club" with Senator John Warner of Virginia, Robertson offered this prayer. The two had discussed the arms race, the huge amounts of money the superpowers were spending on weapons development, and what Warner believed was the imminent threat of nuclear attack by Russian missiles.

"Forbid it, Almighty God!"[130]

PATRICK HENRY

In his impassioned plea to the Virginia Convention in 1775, the orator Patrick Henry invoked the help of God to make the colonies stand firm against England. He reminded the statesmen that they would not fight their battle alone. "There is a just God who presides over the destinies of nations; and who will raise up friends to fight our battles for us. . . ." Henry concluded with his famous declaration, "I know not what course others may take; but as for me, give me liberty, or give me death!"

"Lord, make me an instrument of your peace. Where there is hatred let me sow love, where there is injury, pardon, where there is despair, hope, and where there is sadness, joy. O Divine Master, let me not so much seek to be consoled as to console, to be understood as to understand, to be loved, as to love. For it is in giving that we receive. It is in pardoning that we are pardoned. And it is in dying that we are born to eternal life." [131]

Francis of Assisi

The gentle little monk whose simplicity of faith and life became legend, is said to have visited a Sultan to tell him about Jesus. According to the custom of the day, the Sultan could have had Francis killed, but the fierce ruler was impressed by Francis' courage and honesty. Francis told the Sultan that inner peace would come through prayer and then taught him this prayer.

"What's happening to me? What's wrong? Please help me!"[132]

BETTYE SHELTON

When Bettye Shelton called on God in loneliness and desperation, few would have guessed she could be this unhappy. But in spite of the signs of success, her marriage to country singer Ricky Van Shelton was in shambles. In the moment following her prayer, God answered with a phone call from an acquaintance who felt driven to pray for Bettye. Through this woman, Bettye Shelton found a new relationship with Jesus Christ, and, eventually, with her husband.

"Lord, I'm probably 10,000 miles away from home and my godly parents, grandparents, and my pastor. It's just You and I here. I want to live so badly. It looks like this is the time for me to die. Lord, apparently You can't open this chute." [133]

H.C. Kiser

Over Bologna, Italy, a German antiaircraft shell exploded under a B-17 bomber, sending the plane spiraling. His buddies had all bailed out of the plane before H.C. Kiser decided to jump, wearing the only parachute left—one that was torn. Believing the Lord had directed him to jump, Kiser now prayed for a miracle. Then, with a jerk, the parachute opened and floated to an area away from the bombing target. Kiser was captured by Nazi soldiers, but his Christian faith kept him going for the next seven grueling months before his prison camp was liberated.

"Jesus, I'm giving You this money for Your birthday present."

RYAN FORTH, AGE 3

For several weeks before Christmas, the Forth family gathered loose change and deposited it in a glass Christmas tree container for a Haitian orphanage. As Christmas approached, Ryan and his mother prepared for a shopping trip. Ryan's handful of coins would buy him something special. On impulse, his mother said, "Ryan, you know that when we give money to the orphans it's like giving something to Jesus. Christmas is Jesus' birthday. Would you like to take three of your coins and give them to Jesus for His birthday?" Without a second thought, Ryan picked out three coins, and as he walked over to the glass tree, he made sure Jesus knew what he was doing.

"Lord, here I am. What do You want to say to me?" [134]

EVELYN CHRISTENSON

Author Evelyn Christenson is known for her books and seminars on prayer. For years her first-thing-in-the-morning routine has begun with lying quietly, listening for what the Lord has to say to her for that day. Then she writes down the thoughts that come to her, and puts them in file folders. These thoughts from the Lord become the basis for her writing and speaking.

"My Jesus, I love Thee, I know Thou art mine.
For Thee all the follies of sin I resign;
My gracious Redeemer, my Savior art Thou;
If ever I loved Thee, my Jesus, 'tis now." [135]

TONY CAMPOLO (WILLIAM FEATHERSTONE)

In his book, *Carpe Diem,* Tony Campolo tells how the singing of love songs to Jesus dissipates the doubt that sometimes threatens his faith. "Doubts are conquered, not in philosophical logic or in theological debate, but simply in loving Jesus and in asking Him to love me. In the end it is love that casteth out fears." This well-loved hymn is one Campolo often chooses.

"Thou mastering me
God! giver of breath and bread;
World's strand, sway of the sea;
Lord of living and dead;
Thou hast bound bones and veins in me,
fastened me flesh,
And after it almost unmade, what with dread,
Thy doing: and dost Thou touch me afresh?
Over again I feel Thy finger and find Thee." [136]

Gerard Manley Hopkins

Throughout his life, and even after he was ordained a Jesuit priest, the noted nineteenth century English poet, Gerard Manley Hopkins, was troubled by his inability to give enough of himself to God. For a time he abandoned the writing of poetry and burned much of what he'd written. When a German ship sank, carrying five exiled nuns, he was moved to write one of his greatest poems. The first verse is above.

"Oh, dear God, You know how much we love Sharon, how we long to keep her with us. Thank You for answering my prayer and giving me the assurance, through the movement of her eyelid, that she is aware of my presence . . . I know You love her with a love far beyond our human love, and that even death cannot separate her from You or Your love. That thought comforts me so much now, Lord, and gives me the strength to say 'Thy will be done.'" [137]

LUCILLE GARDNER

Her fifteen-year-old daughter, Sharon, lay in the recovery room following brain surgery, her head and part of her face swathed in bandages. Only hours before she had been hit by a car. Lucille Gardner watched for some sign of life—some sign of recognition from this still figure with tubes and hoses protruding from mouth and nose. Only one eye was visible under a swollen eyelid. "If you can hear me, Sharon, please blink your eyelid," Lucille asked. For just an instant, the eyelid fluttered. This was the beginning of a long and painful journey back to health which called on the faith and courage of both mother and daughter.

"I'm angry at you, God. I wonder, at times, if You even exist. Or if You do exist, do You really care? You say You're closest to people when they need You the most. Well, if that's the case, where are You right now? Why don't You take away my hurt? Where are You, God? Where? Show me that You haven't deserted me, God. I need a sign!"[138]

REUEL NYGAARD

It was the most honest prayer he'd ever prayed. Crushed and broken by the suicide of his twenty-four-year-old son, Reuel Nygaard had retreated with his wife to the quiet of their Minnesota cabin. But this place so loved by the family, was full of memories. Pedaling through a tree-shaded trail, Reuel begged for a sign that God was there. Then around a corner up ahead, on the back of a little trailer pulled by one of a trio of bikes, he saw the words: JESUS IS LORD. His sign. The bikers were Christians, they said, when he'd caught up with them. Two hours later they parted, having shared a nourishing time of fellowship.

"Jesus, lover of my soul, let me to Thy bosom fly, while the waters nearer roll, while the tempest still is high, hide me, O my Savior, hide, till the storm of life is past; safe into the haven glide, O receive my soul at last."[139]

Charles Wesley

Charles Wesley's hymn prayers speak clearly of his intimate relationship with Jesus Christ. Although Charles, an ordained minister like his brother, John, preached at the revival meetings run by his brother and George Whitfield, it was his contribution of music that was notable. It is said that he wrote over 6,000 hymns. Many are still in use today.

"Teach me, Father, to sing again. . . .
Lord, help me to use these golden hours.
The doors to the whole world are open."[140]

INGRID TROBISCH

In her first year of grieving over her husband Walter's sudden death at age fifty-five, Ingrid Trobisch knew she should make no major decisions. But she needed a sense of direction. During a quiet week of renewal near Salzburg, Austria, she wrote a list of priorities, with prayer for God's help in keeping them. She realized that her favorite time of day, the "golden hours" just before and after sunset, could be a time of new life for her.

"May we learn true fear of Thee. May we understand that just as asleep we are as helpless as a baby, so by day we are just as helpless without Thy loving guidance." [141]

Rev. Bob Childress

From the start, there was mutual respect between John Worley, the tall, strapping sheriff known as "King of Slate Mountain," and Bob Childress, the Presbyterian preacher who had returned to the Blue Ridge of his youth. John wasn't ready to become a Christian, but he would sit quietly while Bob prayed. Bob believed that some day the tough, hard-drinking deputy would see the Light. One day he did, and later was ordained a Methodist minister.

"Dear God, we are living at the time of year when it's hard to see over the desk, perhaps even the next hour. In these times of pressure it can also make us short with You, with ourselves, and with each other. May we be given not only the gift of patience, but the gift of grace. And as at times we look back over our lives and find the points where we were short, that we may have an opportunity to go back and speak a word of recognition, apology, or whatever it may be that will bring the fruit of the Spirit to full blossom, even at the times when it's costly and difficult to do so. For in those periods we find once again that Your Word does not return void."

PROFESSOR JOHN WIBORG

At North Park Seminary in Chicago, John Wiborg, professor of systematic theology and worship, is beloved for many reasons. One of them is the extemporaneous prayer he offers before each class. This one was recorded by one of his students.

"Lighten our darkness, we beseech Thee, O Lord; and by Thy great mercy defend us from all perils and dangers of this night; for the love of Thy only Son, our Saviour, Jesus Christ. Amen." [142]

Sheldon Vanauken

The great love of his life, his wife Davy, lay dying, and Sheldon Vanauken prayed a prayer familiar to them both. Then Davy prayed for all the doctors and nurses by name. Theirs had been an uncommon marriage—complete with what they called their "Shining Barrier" against anything that might separate them. Together, they had discovered new life in Jesus Christ through the influence and friendship of C.S. Lewis. Following Davy's death, Lewis continued to be Vanauken's friend throughout his grief, not knowing that in a few years, he would face a similar experience.

"Dear God, the Bible says if we have faith we can move mountains. I don't need any mountains moved. I just need two pairs of shoes moved. Thank You." [143]

MARGARET TWETEN (JENSEN)

Being a pastor's daughter in a Scandinavian settlement in Canada meant having a wardrobe "courtesy of the missionary barrel." That's why young Margaret was horrified when the only shoes for her in the barrel were two pair of the ugly high button variety. Papa was determined she should wear them, for she needed the shoes badly. But certainly if she prayed, God could get rid of these and bring her something better. God didn't move the shoes, but when Margaret wore the ugly shoes to Sunday School, she discovered that one of her classmates had no shoes at all. Margaret learned a valuable lesson about having an obedient and thankful heart.

"Here lie I, Martin Elginbrodde:
Ha'e mercy o' my soul, Lord God,
As I wad do, were I Lord God
And ye were Martin Elginbrodde." [144]

Epitaph in Aberdeen Churchyard

The Scottish author, George MacDonald, first received acclaim with his novels about life in rural Scotland. One of them, *David Elginbrod,* includes this epitaph.

"My Lord, I made this song for You.
To thank You for all what You've done for me.
I know I cannot repay You,
So, Lord, thank You so much.

"In times of pain and in suffering
I turn to You for Your help.
You're always there to help me, Lord.
So, Lord, thank You so much." [145]

MARGARET KAUPUNI

The congregation of Hawaii's Kalihu Union Church listened with tears as a fifty-nine year-old woman, her feet and hands disfigured by leprosy, sang her song of praise. Because of her disease, Margaret Kaupuni spent forty-seven years in exile on the island of Molokai. She lost three husbands to leprosy. Each of her four children was taken from her at birth and put out for adoption. Through all of this, Margaret's profound but simple faith in her Lord brought her, and everyone around her, joy and hope.

"Dear God, what is wrong with me?" [146]

JIM EISENREICH

Jim Eisenreich had finally realized his dream: center field for the Minnesota Twins. But a baffling life-long phenomena threatened that dream. For no discernible reason, his body would jerk as though it had a mind of its own, and he would make guttural, snorting sounds which he could not control. One night playing Boston, the jerking was so bad, Eisenreich ran off the field, begging God for an answer. For the next couple years, conscious of God's presence, Jim learned to live with his condition, diagnosed as a neurological disorder called Tourette Syndrome. Now he is back playing ball and thankful for opportunities to inform the public about this misunderstood disorder.

"Our Father—for we belong to Thee; however cut off from the rest of Thy family we may be. . . . Hallowed be Thy name—nothing is hallowed here. Thy Kingdom come—Already we have spent two years here for Thee, with few signs of a break. . . . Give us this day our daily bread—we are out of eggs and vegetables and there are no shops. . . . And forgive us our trespasses—conditions seem sometimes to bring the worst out of us. . . . Deliver us from evil—rumors of Nosu killing. . . . For thine is the Kingdom, and the power, and the glory—come quickly Lord, and reign."[147]

A.J. BROOMHALL

In 1942, Dr. A.J. Broomhall, nephew of Hudson Taylor, left coastal China to minister to a remote tribe of Nosu. During a particularly discouraging time he wrote this expanded version of the Lord's Prayer. Broomhall later helped pioneer a work among primitive tribes on the island of Mindoro in the Philippines.

". . . by Thy unerring counsel, amid the vicissitudes of life, a lamp to our feet and a light to our path, to love those who despitefully use us . . ."[148]

PAPA HERRING

Lucy Saunders Herring, granddaughter of slaves, grew up in a loving North Carolina home with eleven brothers and sisters. Every Sunday morning when the family gathered for breakfast, her papa prayed—rich and beautiful phrases that stayed in her mind and heart as she grew up and left home. Lucy Herring's determination to do something for her people in an era of chain gangs, lynchings, police abuse, and the Ku Klux Klan, led her to an M.A. from the University of Chicago and fifty-two years as an educator in the South.

"Oh my God . . . I do believe that, I really do. I believed it then and I believe it now. It's been there all the time, hasn't it, packed in my trunk, buried under a bunch of junk." [149]

MARY ELLEN TON

Laughing and crying with joy and relief, Mary Ellen Ton knelt by her bed. Because of the disfiguring burns she'd received in a fire, she had struggled for months with anger, self-pity, fear of the future. Now God had brought her to the place where she could read and accept the words she'd just come across—words she'd scribbled in the margin of a book before the tragic fire: "I believe in God's continuing work in my life and I believe I have within me the possibility to bloom again."

"Oh God, I would rather hear the clods fall on the coffin lid of my child than to hear its cries because it is taken away from me." [150]

SLAVE MOTHER

In the mid-1800s, slave parents were forced to give up their children at the whim of their owners. This mother's baby was sold to another "master" when she and her owners stopped at a boarding house on a journey from Wilmington, Delaware to an unknown destination. The new master ordered one of his slaves to take the crying baby away while the mother sobbed this prayer of abject grief.

"God, Our Loving Father, You gave Your only Son to suffer and to die for me. Grant that when we are found worthy to endure suffering for Christ's name, we may rejoice in our calling and be enabled to bear our part in completing His suffering for the sake of Your church." [151]

Bishop Desmond Tutu (from Anglican prayer calendar)

In 1982 Desmond Tutu spoke for the South African Council of Churches before an austere commission that clearly hoped to discredit the council's work with victims of the South African struggle. Tutu, who was awarded the Nobel Peace Prize two years later, began his submission by demonstrating from Scripture that the council's actions were in obedience to Christ in response to God's Word. He ended with the prayer of the week from the Anglican calendar familiar to Eloff Commission members.

"Stay with me, God. The night is dark, the night is cold: my little spark of courage dies. The night is long; be with me, God, and make me strong." [152]

A SOLDIER'S PRAYER

With the fall of France to the Nazis in World War II, Tunisia, a French holding on the north coast of Africa, became a battleground. During the battle of El Agheila in the Tunisian desert, this prayer, written on a scrap of paper, was found in a trench. Members of the British Eighth Army later published it.

"We pray Thee, O God of might, wisdom, justice, through whom authority is rightly administered, laws are enacted, and judgment decreed, assist with Thy Holy Spirit of counsel and fortitude the President of these United States . . . Let the light of Thy divine wisdom direct the deliberation of Congress . . . May this glorious charter of our civil rights be deeply imprinted on the hearts and memories of our people! . . . May the blessing of Almighty God, Father, Son, and Holy Ghost, descend upon our beloved country and upon all her people and abide with them forever! Amen." [153]

Centennial Prayer James Cardinal Gibbons

In 1876, 100 years after the signing of the Declaration of Independence, Philadelphia was the scene of an exposition to which all the countries of the world were invited. President Ulysses S. Grant and members of Congress attended the grand opening where Cardinal Gibbons offered the prayer.

"Our fathers' God! From out whose hand the centuries fall like grains of sand, we meet today, united, free and loyal to our Lord and Thee to thank Thee for the era done, and trust Thee for the opening one." [154]

Centennial Hymn John Greenleaf Whittier

In his late 60s, Quaker poet John Greenleaf Whittier, was asked to write a hymn commemorating the 1876 Centennial of the United States. No doubt, Whittier's words "united, free" referred not only to freedom from outside rule, but to the results of the abolition of slavery. Before the Civil War, Whittier crusaded for the freedom of slaves, as well as other humanitarian causes.

"We pray that You will hear us as we think about our graduation, even though we have trouble using the traditional language for talking to You and though many of us no longer feel a part of a religious community. . . . Somehow this year more than others we have had to draw lines, to try to find an absolute right with which we could identify ourselves. First in the face of the daily killings and draft calls of the curiously undeclared Vietnam War. Then with the assassinations of Martin Luther King and Senator Kennedy. . . . We pray that you will help us accept the past and face the future with courage and dignity." [155]

SUSANNAH H. WOOD

In 1968, at the Radcliffe College baccalaureate service, a graduating senior offered this prayer.

"God, I cannot go out there." [156]

LEIGHTON FORD

Evangelist Leighton Ford had preached to crowds all over the world when, in 1975, a strange fear almost immobilized him every time he got up to speak. One day, before facing a stadium full of university students, he felt he could not go on. In desperation he fell to his knees and prayed. A verse came to him, "Fear not, I am your shield and your exceeding great reward." Leighton realized that the fear came because so much of his identity and personal acceptance was invested in his speaking ability. God reminded him that His love was unconditional. From that point, Leighton Ford began to work *from* acceptance rather than *toward* acceptance.

"O God, may peace and justice result from the Camp David talks." [157]

INTERNATIONAL "CALL TO PRAYER"

Before President Jimmy Carter, Menachem Begin, and Anwar Sadat met at Camp David in 1978, an important message went out to the world. Rosalynn Carter worked with Jody Powell and Carter's Prayer Breakfast group to draft a statement asking "people of all faiths to pray with us that peace and justice may result from these deliberations." The Camp David deliberations proved to be historic in their results.

"Who am I, O Lord, and to what hast Thou called me, Thou who didst assist me with such divine power that today I constantly exalt and magnify Thy name among the heathens wherever I may be, and not only in good days but also in tribulation." [158]

St. Patrick

The legendary St. Patrick was born in England and captured by Irish marauders when he was sixteen. After several years he escaped, fled to the Continent, and entered a monastery. God led him back to Ireland as a missionary in 432 where he patiently and lovingly evangelized the pagan Irish, tribe by tribe.

". . . we ask Your special blessing for our beloved Queen Wilhelmina on whose shoulders You have laid such a heavy burden. Be her strength so she can guide us according to Your will. But above all, we pray that Your Son may return soon, in all His glory, and that we may be with Him forever, world without end. Amen!" [159]

"OPA" TEN BOOM

One of the tender joys of hiding out in the ten Boom home during World War II, was hearing the dear old father of the house, Caspar ("Opa") ten Boom pray. His snow-white hair and beard gave him the air of a patriarch. His manner indicated that he was well acquainted with the One to whom he prayed. For his resistance activities, Opa was arrested along with his daughters, Corrie and Betsie, in a raid on their home. He died in prison only a few days later.

"Thank You for children
brought into being
because we loved.
God of love
keep us loving
so that they
may grow up whole
in love's overflow." [160]

JOSEPH BAYLY

His poetry is only one of the legacies Joe Bayly left when he died in 1986. For 25 years he wrote a column, "Out of My Mind," for *Eternity Magazine,* fearlessly, but with gentleness and humor, speaking out about the overlooked inconsistencies of the church. Bayly's career began on Ivy League school campuses as an InterVarsity Christian Fellowship staff member, and ended as president of a Christian publishing company.

"Lord, how can our family devotions become more interesting and valuable to my children, and how can I myself learn to read the Bible with more interest?" [161]

KEN TAYLOR

As his children grew out of the Bible story books they read together in evening devotions, Ken Taylor realized it was time they began reading directly from the Bible. But the stilted language of the *King James Version* did not hold the children's attention. Ken asked God for help. It was then that the idea came to paraphrase the Scripture in today's language. His family's enthusiastic response to his first attempts, spurred him on. Sixteen years later, *The Living Bible,* Taylor's paraphrase of the entire Bible, was published. God answered his prayer, not only for his family, but for millions of people around the world.

Precious Lord, take my hand, lead me on, let me stand, I am tired, I am weak, I am worn; thru the storm, thru the night, lead me on to the light, take my hand, precious Lord, lead me home. [162]

THOMAS ANDREW DORSEY

Thomas Andrew Dorsey, the "Father of Gospel Music," began his ministry of music in his home church, the Pilgrim Baptist Church in Chicago where he organized and directed the Gospel choir. Later he helped form the National Convention of Gospel Choirs and Choruses and established his own music publishing company. He wrote this poignant and familiar prayer set to music when both his wife and son died in childbirth.

"God, I'm going to fight this thing.
But ultimately, do with me as You will." [163]

ANN JILLIAN

The highest-rated TV movie of 1987-88 was "The Ann Jillian Story," in which Ann Jillian plays herself. The movie told the true story of Ann's rising career as an actress, her marriage to her manager/husband, Andy, and the cancer that resulted in a double mastectomy in 1985. Ann's relationship with Jesus Christ gave her courage when she most needed it. Shortly before her mastectomy she came to a place of surrender—complete trust in God for whatever he had planned for her.

"Lord, open our eyes
That we may see You in our brothers and sisters.
Lord, open our ears,
That we may hear the cries of the hungry, the cold,
the frightened, the oppressed.
Lord, open our hearts,
that we may love each other as You love us.
Renew in us Your spirit.
Lord, free us and make us one." [164]

MOTHER TERESA

To the world, Mother Teresa's name is synonymous with love and caring. At seventeen she left her home in Albania for India where she became a nun. In 1948 she left the convent in Calcutta to found the Missionaries of Charity. With an uncompromising dedication to the poorest of the poor, especially the "untouchables" of society, Mother Teresa and the sisters of the society now minister in areas around the globe.

"Abba, Father, all things are possible to Thee; remove this cup from Me; yet not what I will but what Thou wilt."

OUR LORD JESUS CHRIST

Jesus referred to God as "Father" 170 times in the four Gospels. In His poignant prayer as He faced crucifixion He used the even more familiar "Abba"—Aramaic for a childlike relationship, like "Papa" or "Daddy." For a Jew to have the audacity to call God "Father" invited more than raised eyebrows. They would not even repeat the name of God. But Jesus introduced His people to a whole new concept of God—as loving, caring parent.

Notes

1. William Mallard, *Language and Love* (University Park, Penn.: Pennsylvania State University Press, 1994), 2.
2. Andrew Murray, *With Christ in the School of Prayer* (Westwood, N.J.: Fleming H. Revell Company, 1958), 185.
3. Elizabeth R. Skoglund, *Amma* (Grand Rapids: Baker Books, 1994), 16.
4. Irving Harris, *The Breeze of the Spirit* (New York: Crossroad/Seabury Press, 1978), 5.
5. Pat Boone, *A Miracle a Day Keeps the Devil Away* (Westwood, N.J.: Fleming H. Revell Company, 1974), 37.
6. Eugenia Price, *Early Will I Seek Thee* (New York: Dial Press, 1983), 36.
7. Edith Deen, *Great Women of the Christian Faith* (New York: Harper & Brothers Publishers, 1959), 126–27.
8. Michael de la Bedoyere, *The Archbishop and the Lady* (New York: Pantheon, 1956), 191.
9. G.A. Williamson, *Foxes Book of Martyrs* (Boston: Little, Brown and Company, 1965), 130.
10. David McCasland, *Oswald Chambers: Abandoned to God* (Grand Rapids: Discovery House, 1993), 35.
11. Rachel Dickerson, "Twenty-six Miles to Run," *Faith at Work,* Spring, 1996.

12. C.S. Lewis, *A Grief Observed* (New York: HarperCollins, 1961), 55.
13. Elisabeth Elliot, *Through Gates of Splendor* (New York: Harper & Row Publishers, 1958), 256.
14. Paul F. Bolles, Jr., *George Washington and Religion* (Dallas: Southern Methodist University Press, 1963), 71.
15. Charles Turner, ed., *Chosen Vessels* (Ann Arbor, Mich: Servant Publications, 1985), 80.
16. John Perkins, *Let Justice Roll Down* (Glendale, Calif.: Regal Books, 1976), 100.
17. David Wilkerson, *The Cross and the Switchblade* (Old Tappan, N.J.: Fleming H. Revell Company, 1963), 10.
18. Kay Kuzma, *Building Your Child's Character From the Inside Out,* (Elgin, Ill.: LifeJourney Books, 1988), 72–73.
19. Deen, *Great Women of the Christian Faith,* 166.
20. McCasland, *Oswald Chambers: Abandoned to God,* 151.
21. Carolyn Koons, *Beyond Betrayal* (San Francisco: Harper & Row Publishers, 1984), 213.
22. Elliot, *Through Gates of Splendor,* 255.
23. *The Book of Common Prayer* (The Seabury Press, 1979), 62.
24. Hans Poley, *Return to the Hiding Place* (Elgin, Ill.: LifeJourney Books, 1993), 140.
25. Richard J. Foster, Prayer, *Finding the Heart's True Home* (New York: HarperCollins Publishers, 1992), 94.
26. Frank C. Laubach, *Learning the Vocabulary of God* (Nashville: Upper Room, 1956), 7.
27. Deen, *Great Women of the Christian Faith* 216.
28. Amanda Smith, *Mrs. Amanda Smith, an Autobiography* (Chicago: AFRO–AM Press, 1969), 245.
29. Sue Monk Kidd, *God's Joyful Surprise* (Harper and Row: San Francisco, 1987), 216.
30. Robert Schuller, *Tough Times Never Last, But Tough People Do* (Nashville: Thomas Nelson Publishers, 1983), 24.

31. Catherine Marshall, *Meeting God at Every Turn* (Lincoln, Va.: Chosen Books, 1980), 77.

32. Horton Davies, ed., *Communion of Saints* (Grand Rapids: Wm. B. Eerdmans Publishing Company, 1990), 112.

33. Benjamin Carson, M.D., *Think Big* (Grand Rapids: Zondervan Publishing House, 1992), 45.

34. Tim Hansel, *When I Relax, I Feel Guilty* (Elgin, Ill.: David C. Cook, 1979), 77.

35. Colleen Townsend Evans and Laura Hobe, *Give Us This Day Our Daily Bread* (Garden City, N.J.: Doubleday & Company, 1981), 81.

36. E. Stanley Jones, *A Song of Ascents* (Nashville: Abingdon Press, 1968), 53.

37. John Greene, "A Most Unusual Request," *Guideposts,* November, 1993.

38. Charles Colson, *Born Again* (Tappan, N.J.: Chosen/Hodder & Stoughton, 1976), 117.

39. James Gilchrist Lawson, *Deeper Experiences of Famous Christians* (Anderson, Ind.: The Warner Press, 1911) 315–16.

40. Marie Henry, *The Secret Life of Hannah Whitall Smith* (Grand Rapids: Zondervan: Grand Rapids, 1984), 105.

41. Schuller, *Tough Times Never Last,* 203.

42. Edwina Gately, *I Hear a Seed Growing* (Trabuco Canyon, Calif.: Source Books, 1990), 95.

43. Gustav Konig, *Life of Martin Luther* (London: Nathaniel Cooke, 1853), 28.

44. Williamson, *Foxes Book of Martyrs,* 72.

45. Hugh T. Kerr and John M. Mulder, ed., *Conversions* (Grand Rapids: Wm. B. Eerdmans Publishing Co., 1983),10.

46. Maria Von Trapp, *Maria* (Wheaton, Ill.: Creation House, 1972), 41.

47. Alice Armstrong Ward with A. Dudley Ward, *I Remain Unvanquished* (Nashville: Abingdon Press, 1970), 138.

48. James Stolpa, "Ordeal in a Frozen Wilderness," *Guideposts,* January, 1994.

49. Marjorie Holmes Mighell, *How Can I Find You, God?* (Carmel, New York: Guideposts Associates/Doubleday, 1975), 118.

50. W.L. Doughty, ed., *The Prayers of Susanna Wesley* (Grand Rapids: Zondervan, 1984), 15.

51. Davies, *Communion of Saints,* 20.

52. Joni Eareckson Tada, *Choices, Changes* (Grand Rapids: Zondervan Publishing House, 1986), 179.

53. Ethel Waters with Charles Samuels, *His Eye Is On the Sparrow* (Garden City, New York: Doubleday & Company, 1950), 270.

54. Foxfire Foundation, *Foxfire 7* (Garden City, New York: Anchor Books, 1982), 55–56

55. Becky Tirabassi, *Releasing God's Power* (Nashville: Thomas Nelson, 1990), 68.

56. Davies, *Communion of Saints,* 36.

57. Deen, *Great Women of the Christian Faith,* 98.

58. Robert Coles, *The Spiritual Life of Children* (Boston: Houghton Mifflin Company, 1990), 50.

59. Dee Dee Risher, "The Way to God," *The Other Side,* November/December, 1995.

60. Earl and Hazel Lee, *The Cycle of Victorious Living* (Kansas City, Mo.: Beacon Hill Press, 1971), 37.

61. Davies, *Communion of Saints,* 32

62. Ibid., 43.

63. Beth Jameson, *Hold Me Tight* (Old Tappan, N.J.: Fleming H. Revell Company, 1980), 75.

64. Arnold Prater, *Prayer Partners* (Nashville: Abingdon Press, 1987), 39.

65. Rev. Alfred Plummer, *English Church History* (Edinburgh: T. & T. Clark, 1904), 166.

66. Arnold Dallimore, *Spurgeon* (Chicago: Moody Press, 1984), 23.

67. Johnny Cash, *Man in Black* (Grand Rapids: Zondervan, 1975), 161.

68. Jimmy Carter and Rosalynn Carter, *Everything to Gain* (New York: Random House, 1987), 22.

69. Corrie ten Boom and Jamie Buckingham, *Tramp for the Lord* (Old Tappan, N.J.: Christian Literature Crusade/Fleming H. Revell, 1974), 57.

70. Davies, *Communion of Saints,* 84.

71. Roland H. Bainton, *Women of the Reformation in France and England* (Minneapolis: Augsburg Publishing House, 1973), 188–89.

72. John D. Pierce, "Pitcher's Family Faced Adversity Buoyed by Faith and the Faithful," *Baptist Press,* 1995.

73. Ed Rowell, "Injuries Propel Bull Rider to Renew Relationship with God," *Baptist Press,* 1995.

74. Ana Gascon Ivey, "Down in the Dumps in Guatemala," *Clarity,* July/August, 1994.

75. Walter Wangerin, Jr., *As For Me and My House* (Nashville: Thomas Nelson, 1987), 21.

76. Jim Castelli, *How I Pray* (New York: Ballantine Books, 1994), 40.

77. Dag Hammarskjold, *Markings* (London: Faber & Faber, 1964), 93.

78. John N. Wall, Jr., Ed., *George Herbert, The Country Parson, The Temple* (New York: Paulist Press, 1981), 245.

79. F. Kefa Sempangi, *A Distant Grief* (Glendale, Calif.: Regal Books, 1979), 120–21.

80. Williamson, *Foxes Book of Martyrs,* 131.

81. Joan Winmill Brown, ed., *The Martyred Christian* (New York: Macmillan Publishing Co., 1983), 171.

82. Jeb Stuart Magruder, *From Power to Peace* (Waco, Texas: Word, 1978), 158.

83. Robert Van de Weyer, *The Harper/Collins Book of Prayers* (San Francisco: Harper/Collins, 1993), 315.

84. *Foxfire 7,* 40.

85. Ibid., 45
86. Caroline Stickley, *Broken Snare* (London: Overseas Missionary Fellowship, 1975), 198.
87. Terry Whalin and Chris Woehr, *One Bright Shining Path* (Wheaton, Ill.: Crossway Books, 1993), 23.
88. James and Marti Hefley, *The Church That Takes on Trouble* (Elgin, Ill.: David C. Cook, 1976), 193.
89. Elizabeth O'Connor, *Call to Commitment* (New York: Harper & Row Publishers, 1963), 59.
90. Doris Elaine Fell, *Lady of the Tboli* (Chappaqua, New York: Christian Herald Books, 1979), 62.
91. Edward Hays, *Pray All Ways* (Leavenworth, Kan.: Forest of Peace Books, 1981), 49.
92. Bill Milliken, *So Long, Sweet Jesus* (New York: Prometheus Press, 1973), 159.
93. *The HarperCollins Book of Prayers,* 348.
94. James Anthony Froude, *Bunyan* (London: MacMillan & Co., 1902), 49.
95. *Foxfire 7,* 211
96. Dr. Larry Crabb, Jr. and Lawrence Crabb, Sr., *God of My Father* (Grand Rapids: Zondervan Publishing House, 1994), 41, 148.
97. Kerr and Mulder, *Conversions,* 152.
98. Stanley High, *Billy Graham* (New York: McGraw Hill, 1956), 115.
99. Lauren Homer, "To Russia with Love," *Guideposts,* August, 1994.
100. Robert Ellsberg, ed., *By Little and By Little* (New York: Alfred A. Knopf, 1983), 21.
101. Charles L. Wallis, *Autobiography of Peter Cartwright* (New York/ Nashville: Abingdon Press, 1956), 37.
102. Francis W. Vanderwall, *Water in the Wilderness* (Mahwah, N.J.: Paulist Press, 1985), 25.
103. Etty Hillesum, *An Interrupted Life* (New York: Pantheon, 1984), 151.

104. William P. Mahedy, *Out of the Night* (New York: Ballantine/Epiphany Books, 1986), 229.

105. Diana Dewar, *All for Christ* (Oxford, England: Oxford University Press, 1980), 98–99.

106. Marcia and Jack Kelly, *One Hundred Graces* (Bell Tower/Harmony, 1992), 77.

107. Ruth Bell Graham, *It's My Turn* (Old Tappan, N.J.: Fleming H. Revell Company, 1982), 56.

108. Keith Miller and Bruce Larson, *Living the Adventure* (Waco, Texas: Word Books, 1975), 77.

109. Rosell and Dupois, ed., *Memoirs of Charles G. Finney* (Grand Rapids: Zondervan, 1989), 20.

110. W. Garden Blaikie, *The Personal Life of David Livingstone* (New York: Laymen's Missionary Movement, 1910), 453.

111. Ike Keay, *Child of Pain, Children of Joy* (Old Tappan, N.J.: Fleming H. Revell Company, 1989), 19.

112. Madeleine L'Engle, *A Circle of Quiet* (New York: Farrar, Straus & Giroux, 1972), 228.

113. Karen Burton Mains, *Karen! Karen!* (Wheaton, Ill.: Tyndale House Publishers, 1979), 103.

114. Evelyn Christenson, *A Journey into Prayer* (Wheaton, Ill.: Victor Books, 1995), 157.

115. Mark Moring, "School Moms, Prayer Warriors," *Christianity Today*, 1995.

116. Gigi Graham Tchividjian, *Sincerely, Gigi* (Grand Rapids: Zondervan Publishing Company, 1984), 109.

117. Reinhold Kerstan, *Blood and Honor* (Elgin, Ill.: David C. Cook, 1980), 66.

118. Char Meredith, *It's a Sin to Bore a Kid* (Word Books: Waco, Texas, 1978), 78.

119. Francis Thompson, *The Hound of Heaven* (Peter Pauper Press), 18.

120. Tim Hansel, *When I Relax, I Feel Guilty* (Elgin, Ill.: David C. Cook, 1979), 25.

121. Kerr and Mulder, *Conversions,* 10.

122. Bob Stewart, Frank Morris, and Elizabeth Morris, *Revenge Redeemed* (Tarrytown, New York: Fleming H. Revell Company, 1991), 199.

123. Bridget Mary Meehan, *Praying with Passionate Women* (New York: Crossroad Publishing Company, 1995), 87–88.

124. James R. Brockman, *The Word Remains: A Life of Oscar Romero* (Maryknoll, New York: Orbis Books, 1982), 207.

125. Malcolm Muggeridge, *Jesus Rediscovered* (Garden City, New York: Doubleday & Company, 1969), 50–51.

126. Art Toalston, David Winfrey, "Prayer Quietly Contributed to Bosnian Peace Agreement," *Baptist Press,* 1995.

127. Kerr and Mulder, *Conversions,* 162.

128. Emile Cailliet and John C. Blankenagel, trans., *Great Shorter Works of Pascal* (Philadelphia: Westminster Press, 1948), 220–21.

129. Flo Conway and Jim Siegelman, *Holy Terror* (New York: Doubleday and Company, 1982), 69.

130. John Bartlett, *Familiar Quotations* (Boston: Little, Brown and Company, 1968), 465.

131. Murray Bodo, *Francis, The Journey and the Dream* (Cincinnati: St. Anthony Messenger Press, 1972), 89.

132. Chip Alford, "Friend, Faith Restored Marriage to Country Singer," *Baptist Press,* 1995.

133. Kellie Crowe, "Christmas in '45: God Reshaped His World Via Burning Bomber, Nazi Prison," *Baptist Press,* 1995.

134. Evelyn Christenson, *A Journey into Prayer* (Wheaton, Ill.: Victor Books, 1995), 40.

135. Tony Campolo, *Carpe Diem* (Dallas: Word Books, 1994), 77.

136. Bartlett, *Familiar Quotations,* 802.

137. Lucille Gardner, *There Is Hope* (Elgin, Ill.: David C. Cook, 1976), 27.

138. Reuel A. Nygaard, *Tragedy to Triumph* (Elgin, Ill.: LifeJourney Books, 1994), 157.

139. Charles Wesley, "Jesus, Lover of My Soul," *Hymns and Sacred Poems,* 1740.

140. Ingrid Trobisch, *Learning to Walk Alone* (Ann Arbor: Servant Books, 1985), 57–58.

141. Richard C. Davis, *The Man Who Moved a Mountain* (Philadelphia: Fortress Press, 1970), 199–200.

142. Sheldon Vanauken, *A Severe Mercy* (New York: Harper & Row, 1977), 175.

143. Margaret Tweten Jensen, *First We Have Coffee* (San Bernardino, Calif.: Here's Life Publishers, 1982), 61.

144. George MacDonald, *David Elginbrod* (New York: Lovell, Caryell, and Co., 1862), 68.

145. Mel White, *Margaret of Molokai* (Waco, Texas: Word Books, 1981), 185–86.

146. Jim Eisenreich, "Never More Than I Can Handle," *Guideposts,* June, 1994.

147. A.J. Broomhall, *Strong Man's Prey* (London: China Inland Mission, 1953), 220–22.

148. Lucy Saunders Herring, *Strangers No More* (New York: Carlton Press, 1993), 14.

149. Mary Ellen Ton, *The Flames Shall Not Consume You* (Elgin, Ill.: David C. Cook, 1982), 136.

150. James Melvin Washington, ed., *Conversations with God: Two Centuries of Prayers by African Christians* (New York: HarperCollins, 1994), 41.

151. Desmond Tutu, *Hope and Suffering* (Grand Rapids: William B. Eerdmans Publishing Co., 1983), 187.

152. Bartlett, *Familiar Quotations,* 1103.

153. *Stepping Stones to Literature* (New York: Silver, Burdett & Company, 1898), 204–5.

154. Ibid., 202.

155. Susannah H. Wood, "A Commencement Prayer," *New York Times Company,* 1968.

156. Norman B. Rohrer and Leighton Ford, *A Life Surprised* (Wheaton, Ill.: Tyndale House Publishers, 1981), 136.

157. Rosalynn Carter, *First Lady From Plains* (Boston: Houghton Mifflin Company, 1984), 245.

158. Paul Gallico, *The Steadfast Man, A Life of St. Patrick* (London: Joseph Ltd., 1958), 216.

159. Hans Poley, *Return to the Hiding Place*, 18.

160. Joseph Bayly, *Psalms of My Life* (Elgin, Ill.: LifeJourney Books, 1987), 66.

161. Ken Taylor, *My Life: A Guided Tour* (Wheaton, Ill.: Tyndale House Publishers, 1991), 210.

162. *Conversations with God: Two Centuries of Prayers by African Christians,* 154.

163. Bernie Sheahan, "Out of the Night," *Aspire,* December, 1994/January, 1995.

165. *The HarperCollins Book of Prayers,* 351.

Index